MECHANIZATION
AND MISERY

Titles of related interest available from Ryburn Publishing include:

Town and City Histories: Bradford
by David James

Victorian Bradford The Living Past
Photography by Ian Beesley Commentary by David James

Undercliffe: Bradford's Historic Victorian Cemetery
Photography by Ian Beesley Commentary by David James

Bradford and the Industrial Revolution
An economic history 1760–1840
by Gary Firth

Bingley in Old Picture Postcards
by Gary Firth

The Ryburn Map of Victorian Bradford
Text by Elvira Willmott

RYBURN ARCHIVE EDITIONS

❦

MECHANIZATION AND MISERY

THE BRADFORD WOOLCOMBERS' REPORT OF 1845

Introduction by J. A. Jowitt

Ryburn Publishing

First published in 1991
Ryburn Publishing Limited
Krumlin, Halifax, England

Introduction © J. A. Jowitt 1991

Jacket designed by Alexander Ferguson at Ryburn Design
Composed by Ryburn Publishing Services
Printed by Ryburn Book Production
Luddendenfoot, Halifax, England

Mechanization and Misery   ISBN 1-85331-012-3

Contents

Preface

With the wholesale demise of their staple industries, the northern industrial areas of the United Kingdom came to recognise, in the 1980s, the difficulties and hardships involved in industrial restructuring. Textiles, coal mining, mechanical engineering, ship building and iron and steel production have all suffered the consequences of structural change. During the last thirty years the landscape of the Yorkshire and Lancashire mill districts has been fundamentally transformed and that most distinctive feature of the Victorian textile sky-line, the mill chimney, has now almost completely disappeared, marking the decline of an industry which, for more than a century, dominated those cities, towns and villages and the lives of their inhabitants. Bradford provides a classic example of this process, for in many ways it acted as the hub of the West Yorkshire wool trade. In the nineteenth and early twentieth centuries it was the international capital of the worsted industry, and as late as 1960 more than 30% of the labour force were still working in textiles. Since that date the industry has collapsed in the face of competition from Third World Countries, from the remodelled textile production of the USA and Europe (most noticeably Italy), and from Central Government's supreme indifference to its fate.

That process has brought in its wake unemployment, poverty and deprivation. Economic restructuring has produced social dislocations, and although these are in a very different context, they bear some resemblance to those which the textile workers experienced in the first half of the nineteenth century when worsted production was mechanized and transformed from a domestic hand trade into a factory-based mechanized industry.

This book looks at the changing fortunes of one group of workers – the woolcombers – within the context of the development of the West Yorkshire worsted industry and its capital, the city of Bradford. At its heart is a reprint of one of the most interesting and enlightening local documents of the period – the Woolcombers' Report of 1845.

For permission to reprint the Woolcombers' Report I am grateful to the Borthwick Institute of Historical Research at York. Many of my other debts, accumulated over many years of research in local and regional history, cannot be fully acknowledged because of space limitations, but special mention needs to be made of a number of people and organisations. David James, the Bradford District Archivist, has facilitated the reprinting, but more importantly has been a continuing source of support and encouragement. To the staff of the Bradford District Archives and those involved with local history materials at Bradford Central Library I owe a debt which can never be repaid; to the late Jack Reynolds for first outlining the history of the woolcombers and for encouraging the belief that the ordinary men and women of Bradford were always its greatest wealth and the greatest source of interest in local studies. To Anne Hull for the space and protection to research and write. Finally to Margaret, Annette, Michael, Joachim and Laura for putting up with missed days in Marsden.

J. A. JOWITT
Bradford 1991

Mechanization and Misery: The Woolcombers

In the course of last week, I have visited some of the most filthy and wretched abodes that the mind of man can conceive, in which misery of the lowest description was personified. In a portion of this town called the Leys, there are scores of wretched hovels, unfurnished and unventilated, damp, filthy in the extreme, and surrounded by stagnant pools, human excrement and every-thing offensive and disgusting to 'sight and smell'. No sewers, no drainage, no ventilation. Nothing to be seen but squalid wretchedness on every side, and the features of the inmates show forth a perfect and unmistakeable index of their condition: all this is to be seen in the centre of this wealthy emporium of the worsted trade.[1]

Between 1800 and 1850 Bradford was transformed from a minor market town and cloth-producing community, into the international worsted textile capital. It became in the process one of the wonders of the world, a magnet for travellers and commentators coming to see the first urban-industrial communities which were mushrooming in the foothills of the Pennines in Yorkshire and Lancashire. The imposing statistics of that transition have often been recounted – of the one small spinning mill in 1800 growing to 129 in 1850; of a spiralling population, increasing from 13,000 inhabitants in 1801 to more than 100,000 in 1851, representing population growth rates of more than 50% in the 1820s, '30s and '40s; the transition from a place of 'purling trout streams and quiet country lanes' to what one public health expert described as 'the dirtiest, filthiest place he had ever visited'.[2] However these descriptions, in particular those cataloguing massive economic growth, were often the product of an intense local pride. The writers wished to emphasize the particular importance of their own community over and above those of other towns and cities, especially their neighbours with whom there was an intense local rivalry. John James, the historian of the worsted trade and of Bradford, waxed eloquent about the transition:

The Metropolis of the Worsted Trade, its hundred streets stretching their wide arms for miles, filled with an overflowing population of busy merchants and manufacturers, artizans and operatives; and the immense products of its stupendous mills – where thousands of clacking power looms, and whirring spinning frames, din the ear – exported to almost every civilized place of the globe.[3]

Descriptions such as these tend to sanitize the processes of industrialization and urbanization, almost disregarding the massive disruption and hardship involved. In the process they often fail to illuminate its impact on individuals and groups, on masters and workers.

Historians have for decades argued whether the coming of mechanized industry and its concentration in an urban environment created overall benefits or whether it brought in its wake misery for millions. This controversy, 'the Standard of Living Debate', has in general reached a consensus that in the long term industrialization and urbanization brought immense benefits for mankind, and that even in the short term the benefits probably outweighed the disadvantages.[4] However, even the most optimistic of these historians has recognised that significant groups were losers in the process of mechanization. At the top of any list of losers were the textile hand workers, in particular the hand weavers and hand combers, whose jobs and livelihoods were swept away by machinery and the factory.

Too often, however, they have been seen simply as an isolated appendix of hardship, a collection of unfortunate but misguided individuals who could not or would not respond to a changing environment. This type of analysis however, fails to understand the sheer quantity of handworkers in the West Riding of Yorkshire in the first half of the nineteenth century, for they constituted the largest single sector of the labour force. It also fails to understand that textile mechanization did not simply occur at one particular moment, but that it took place over more than fifty years.

Innovation occurred in different sectors of the industry at different times and the sectoral nature of mechanization often compounded the problems of the hand workers. So the early mechanization of spinning produced a huge increase in spun yarn and consequently a huge increase in hand combers and weavers, which meant that these groups were inflated in size when they in turn were threatened by the next wave of mechanization.

The hardship experienced by the hand weavers in the 1830s and '40s was, at the time, a source of great controversy and public debate, with parliamentary commissions examining their plight.[5] However, the hand combers have never received such attention either at the time or since. The reasons for this curious omission would seem to lie in the much smaller numbers of hand combers compared with the weavers, and also their absence from the cotton and woollen industries. The hand combers were only engaged in worsted production and by the 1830s and 1840s they were almost entirely concentrated in Bradford, with smaller numbers in Halifax and Keighley and the small textile village communities such as Addingham and Oxenhope. Also the combers signally failed to garner the public sympathy that was bestowed on the hand weavers. Like car workers or dockers in the 1960s, they were a working group who had a bad public image. The reasons for this hostility seem to have been due to their earlier militancy, to their dangerous concentration as a discontented group within one community, and, in the later stages, because of the large number of Irish amongst their numbers.

In the mid 1840s the plight of the hand combers was such that their abject status could not be ignored. Reports of their appalling working conditions, of their poverty and the danger to public health of their situation began to circulate in the local press. But, unlike the weavers whose cause was taken up by parliamentarians and others, the true conditions of the hand combers had to be outlined by the combers themselves. In 1845 they produced one of the classic social surveys of the period, the Woolcombers' Report, which outlined in close and lurid detail the actual conditions under which they lived and worked. That report is here re-published in its entirety, and it can and does stand on its own as a superb survey of a dying trade. However, this critical introduction to the Report hopes to place it in the general context of the mechanization of the worsted textile industry and in the historical development of Bradford.

The Report can be looked at from a number of different perspectives. First and most important it catalogues the plight of a hand trade in the age of mechanization. It outlines the environmental and social conditions that epitomised the early industrial community, and in particular it describes in the starkest form the state of public health which was so bad in Bradford in the 1840s that the average age of death in 1840 was 18.69 years and amongst woolcombers it dipped to below 15. The Report tells us a great deal about the Irish immigrant community, for cross referencing with the 1851 Census Enumerators' books shows how strongly the Irish featured in it. It is an indispensable aid in any attempt to understand the tortuous and confused political situation in the 1840s, which in Bradford was marked by a vitriolic confrontation between Tories and Liberals, between Anglicans and Nonconformists, and between both of them and Irish Catholics. It is also useful in understanding why Bradford was so heavily involved with militant Chartism and why in 1848 it was the centre of physical force Chartism in the United Kingdom.

The Report acts as the source from which a wider analysis of a community in the age of mechanization can be undertaken, and because Bradford was such a classic early industrial community, it is possible draw wider conclusions about the impact of industrialization and urbanization on working men, women and children in Britain in the second quarter of the nineteenth century.

To understand how far the hand combers had fallen by the 1840s it is necessary to go back to the eighteenth century. During the early eighteenth century the British worsted industry developed, expanded and became concentrated on the West Riding of Yorkshire.[6] Prior to that the staple textile trade of the area was woollen cloth production. The woollen trade was organised with a mass of small producers who purchased raw wool and, in their own homes with the labour of the whole family, they carded, spun and wove rough woollen cloth. The cloth was purchased by merchants who finished it in processes such as fulling, shearing and dyeing. From the outset the worsted trade was dominated by a small number of merchants or woolstaplers who purchased the raw wool and then put it out to an army of domestic hand workers. This resulted from its later introduction, its use of the rarer and more expensive long stapled wool and because it did not require the expensive finishing processes associated with woollen cloth production. From its beginnings then the trade rested

> on a much more capitalistic basis than was the case in the woollen trade. The small independent clothier never existed in the worsted industry. . . . The worsted master was usually a large employer with a flock of workpeople at his command . . . in the woollen trade a large number of small men, in the worsted a small number of big men.[7]

So the worsted trade was not composed of independent workers working on their own materials, but rather an army of domestic wage labourers or, as one historian has put it, 'an army of wage dependent domestic workers who virtually formed a rural-industrial proletariat'.[8]

The combers were the élite of the pre-industrial labour force. Using a pair of heavy metallic combs which they heated and reheated in a charcoal fire, they separated the 'tops' – the long fibres needed for worsted spinning – from the 'noils' – the short fibres which were a by-product sold off to the woollen manufacturer. Their power and importance was conferred partly by the nature of their work, but also by a powerful tradition of organization which led to a national union which enforced uniform wage rates and apprenticeship regulations. The independence of the combers is best expressed in John Nicholson's poem:

> The comber next employs his ancient art,
> Which no machinery can supersede.
> In vain the ingenious stretch their utmost skill;
> As oft as tried, the expensive schemes of art
> Abortive prove; – the comber still employed,
> Sings at his work, and triumphs o'er them all;
> Then plans for ale, and when the quart goes round,
> Talks of his travels, happier than a king.[9]

Their power was viewed with distaste by the leaders of the industry and later spokesmen and historians of the trade stigmatised them as

> A discontented race, forever combining against their employers and resorting to extreme methods of coercion and restriction.[10]

However, during the second half of the eighteenth century two important changes occurred which were to have a dramatic long-term effect on the hand combers. The first was the introduction of the Worsted Acts, which gave the worsted masters an immense power over their workforce.[11]

One of the great problems faced by the worsted merchants was the supervision of their domestic workers. Wool was put out throughout the length and breadth of Yorkshire and even further afield, and it was clearly impossible for the employers to supervise working operations. In addition there was considerable natural wastage in worsted production and worsted merchants came to believe that they were being embezzled of their wool. They therefore obtained from Parliament the right to use the rebate on the Soap Duty (a sort of eighteenth century VAT) to set up a Worsted Committee consisting of the major employers who then engaged an Inspectorate to undertake a number of duties. Their main role was to act as an industrial police force and their powers were undoubtedly greatly enhanced because the normal principle of innocent until proven guilty was reversed. Under the Worsted Acts it was the accused who had to prove their innocence, an extremely hard thing to do due to the difficulties of differentiating between legitimate waste and embezzled wool. From the outset the Worsted Acts were aimed at militant workers and the records show that it was primarily used against the combers and against specific individuals who were charged on a number of occasions. Undoubtedly it was used to cow the labour force and it gave the worsted employers a power and strength which was not to be found in the other textile trades. Almost from the inception of the Worsted Acts the powerful position of the combers began to break down.

The second factor, which was of immense importance, was the coming of mechanization. From the 1780s merchants began to recognise that the spinning machinery introduced into the cotton industry – in particular a modification of Richard Arkwright's Water Frame, the Throstle – could be used in worsted spinning. Machine spinning was rapidly introduced into the West Riding worsted textile industry in the face of little or no opposition. This was because spinning was usually associated with women and children, and because the expansion of hand spinning had been retarded; it took between four and six spinners to supply enough yarn to keep one weaver in work and eighteen spinners and weavers to supply one comber. The subsequent increase in spun yarn produced an initial bonanza for the other hand workers. So in the immediate aftermath of the introduction of factory-based machine spinning there was a large scale increase in the overall numbers of hand weavers and combers.

Mechanization also had a major impact on the location of hand combing. As the centre of machine spinning increasingly became concentrated on Bradford, so did hand woolcombing. So whereas hand weaving remained spread throughout the area in countless upland villages, combing became concentrated in one place. In the period between 1800 and 1825 it would seem that the hand combers, although they lost the bulk of their pre-industrial craft prerogatives, managed to retain a generally good position through the overall increase in activity in the trade.

1825 was a major turning point in Bradford's history. In that year the respective strengths of the old and new systems were starkly displayed. At the beginning of the year the Worsted Trade celebrated in a grandiose and flamboyant style the Bishop Blaize festival. This was a seven-yearly public display of communal solidarity in support of the patron saint of the combers. It brought together all in the trade, masters and workers. The descriptions of the procession and the ensuing celebrations indicated a booming industry in which there seemed to be little or no conflict. However, within a matter of months that communal solidarity was shattered by the onset of the 'Great Bradford Strike', a 23-week-long epic in Bradford labour history which shattered the public accord, pitted masters against workers and ushered in a 25-year period of class confrontation and bitterness. The dispute, ostensibly about demands from the hand weavers and combers for an increase in wages, became transformed into a much wider confrontation about the nature of the trade and who controlled it. Its importance was clearly recognised by both sides as employers and trade unionists throughout the United Kingdom attempted to aid each side through collections and the blacklisting of strikers.[12]

The defeat of the strikers transformed the power balance within the trade and opened up a period of employer *Diktat* which saw the immediate introduction of power looms and cuts in wages. For the hand weavers, the largest category of workers in the West Riding, it brought a twenty-year period of

intense suffering as power looms gradually replaced hand workers. In some respects the slow introduction of power looms brought an even greater hardship. Power looms did not produce the huge technological transition and massive immediate economic benefit that was the case with machine spinning and, subsequently, machine combing. In such a situation power and hand looms operated side by side for a long time, allowing textile masters to utilise hand weavers as an economic regulator.

Throughout the second quarter of the nineteenth century the British economy – and in particular its only mechanized sector, the textile trades – was bedevilled by an extreme instability. It fluctuated between boom and slump in a three year cycle of great intensity and, faced by such unstable economic conditions, employers invested to a limited extent in power looms which in periods of boom they supplemented by taking on hand weavers. When the slump came they kept their costly capital equipment running and laid off the hand workers. So, as the number of power looms gradually increased, the hand weavers endured a downward spiral in their wages and a decline in the overall work available.

But the impact of mechanization in weaving had a powerful knock-on effect on combing. As opportunities and conditions declined in hand weaving, the hand weavers turned to the last haven of hand work in the industry – combing. This movement can be seen very clearly in the small textile community of Oxenhope where the number of hand weavers declined from 154 to 87 between the 1841 and 1851 censuses, whilst the number of hand combers rose from 138 to 196.[13] Very rapidly that trade became overstaffed, and this situation was compounded with the arrival of significant numbers of Irish immigrants into Bradford from the late 1830s. These migrants primarily came from the Western counties of Sligo and Mayo and from the midland county of Queens County (present day Laois). The latter were often hand textile workers whose own textile industry had been ruined by British competition after the Act of Union in 1801. For them the obvious source of employment was in hand combing, and by the mid 1840s probably half of the Bradford woolcombers were Irish.[14] The decline in living standards amongst the woolcombers is difficult to quantify due to the different kinds of work undertaken, the different fibres worked upon and the different rates paid by different firms, but contemporary evidence suggests that during the 1830s wages fell by almost two-thirds and that this rate of decline continued in the 1840s.

The biggest problem confronting textile mechanization was the development of machinery to comb wool. Throughout the late 1830s and early 1840s a number of people attempted to develop machinery for combing, recognising the fortune that could be garnered from such an innovation. The key figure in the process was Samuel Cunliffe Lister who, largely through a purchasing of patents, finally developed in the mid 1840s the Lister Nip Comb. That machine signed the death warrant of the combers, for it was estimated by Henry Ripley, the great Bowling dyeing magnate, that one machine comb could replace 100 hand combers;[15] and others estimated that the machine comb reduced the cost of tops from about two shillings (10p) per pound to 4d (1½p). The impact of introducing the Lister Nip Comb was immediate. Within five years half the estimated 10,000 hand combers in Bradford had disappeared from the trade, and although pockets of hand combing endured during the 1850s, it was clear to both masters and workers that they were an obsolete entity. In 1854 a local survey found 2567 combers in Bradford but of these only 700 (27%) were working full-time, 1017 (40%) were occasionally in work and 850 (33%) had no work.[16]

But the predicament of the combers superseded the introduction of machine combing. During the early 1840s their position had become synonymous with poverty, disease and death. There were too many workers in the trade, which saw a constant decline in wages. Further, the combers were increasingly forced to ply their noxious trade within their own homes. Previously much of the combing carried out in Bradford had been conducted in combing shops, but throughout the period employers increasingly dispensed with these. The combers therefore had to use their living quarters to carry on their trade. This involved having a charcoal or coal fire to heat the combs which produced noxious fumes within the home. In addition, as the Bradford trade developed in the 1830s and '40s, it utilised a whole range of new fibres such as alpaca, angora, Indian goat hair and mohair, and these introduced the problem of anthrax. Black alpaca combing, in particular, had an unenviable reputation due to the noxious nature of the fleeces.

How could the combers respond to their worsening situation? Essentially a number of different strategies were employed. The first was to try to use their economic muscle by such means as strikes. Between 1843 and 1845 the combers developed a trade union which embarked on a series of strikes, though by 1846 George White was publicly pronouncing its obituary. But this option had little chance of success, as all the strong cards lay with the masters. The second strategy was to join in political campaigns which would give the working man the vote and which, in turn, could be used to change the situation through the banning or taxing of machinery. From the outset, therefore, combers were particularly associated with the Chartist movement, and throughout the 1840s – particularly in the latter period of 1847 and 1848 – they were the backbone of the Bradford Chartist movement.

The Chartist movement throughout the 1840s was divided between what historians have called the physical force and the moral force wings. The latter – particularly associated with skilled workers and craftsmen – saw its role as bringing about peaceful political change through public meetings, petitions and an educative process that embraced both the movement and the authorities. The other wing of the movement, the physical force Chartists, was overwhelmingly powerful in Bradford. It garnered the hand workers and offered other alternatives. Physical force Chartism in Bradford – increasingly an Irish movement and dominated by Feargus O'Connor especially – was anti-industrial in perspective. It looked back to a happier period before the coming of machines and factories when independent craftsmen cultivated their own small holdings. There was undoubtedly an element of romanticism in this viewpoint, with distance tending to idealize the earlier situation. This romantic, idealized version of the past was well expressed by Frederick Engels when he wrote:

> So the workers vegetated through a passably comfortable existence, leading a righteous and peaceful life in all piety and probity: and their material position was far better than that of their successors. They did not need to overwork; they did no more than they chose to do, and yet earned what they needed. They had leisure for healthful work in garden or field, work which, in itself, was recreation for them, and they could take part besides in the recreations and games of their neighbours.[17]

The Bradford Chartists, dominated by the combers, were major supporters of the Chartist Land Scheme, an attempt to resettle hand workers back on the land. Almost half of the 806 Bradford people involved with Chartist Land resettlement were combers. They were also the predominant element in the attempts at insurrection in 1848, recent evidence suggesting that this was an Anglo-Irish attempt to overthrow the government and to achieve Irish independence.[18]

Another strategy developed by the leaders of the woolcombers was an attempted alliance in an overall anti-industrial coalition with others in Bradford, in particular the old Tory élite. It was in this context that the Woolcombers Report was produced. From 1825 there had been three political factions in Bradford. One group included the factory masters and the middle classes whose position was built on the new industrial system, who were concentrated in the Liberal party and who were often members of the Nonconformist sects, in particular Baptists and Congregationalists. A second grouping was the old élite who had run the town before the coming of industry and in the early stages of the factory community, they were predominantly Tories and associated with the Church of England. These two groups were deeply hostile to each other, their hostility having been exacerbated by the role of Richard Oastler who tried to develop a Tory/Radical anti-industrial alliance. The Tories argued that the coming of the factory had broken down the natural social relationships that had existed prior to industrialization. They therefore strongly urged the state to intervene to control industry, especially with regard to hours of work. Richard Oastler, in his famous letter to the *Leeds Mercury* 'about those magazines of British infantile slavery, the worsted mills of the town and neighbourhood of Bradford', set the tone of this division. In his letter he painted the picture of a poor shoeless factory waif walking to the factory on a cold, wet and windy early morning. Handbills from the previous night's political meeting, attended by all the factory masters and called to protest against the injustice of slavery on the West Indian plantations, lapped round his legs. Oastler drew attention to the hypocrisy of those who condemned slavery on the sugar plantations but who were willing to work seven-year-olds for fourteen hours a day.

There therefore developed within the West Riding of Yorkshire a Tory/Radical alliance which saw the factory master as the ogre of society and the unrestrained factory as a destructive agency causing economic hardship and political and social instability. It was in many ways a curious movement incorporating as it did old-fashioned Tories such as Oastler, Anglican clergymen such as Parson Bull of Bierley and working-class Radical leaders such as Peter Bussey. Above all it was an emotional movement vainly trying to beat back the incoming tide of industrialization. By the late 1830s, with the development of the Chartist movement, it seemed that the heyday of the alliance was over. Chartism had broken both the dichotomy between social and political reform and the pattern of dependence on social superiors for leadership. The Tories had been identified as leaders in social reform movements like factory reform and anti-Poor Law agitation, and the Liberals as leaders in political reform and the extension of the franchise. As an independent working-class movement, Chartism seemed to break that division and combined in one movement the demand for both social and political change. However, the alliance between the Tories and the working classes was to have one last fling in the 1840s, which resulted in the production of the Woolcombers' Report.

That this happened was largely due to two individuals – the first was George White, the comber's leader, and the second was the vicar of Bradford, the Reverend William Scoresby. George White was a dominating figure amongst the woolcombers in a variety of forms. He was heavily involved with attempts at trade unionism, he was a leading physical force Chartist who suffered a number of prison sentences for his beliefs and, in the mid 1840s he became increasingly concerned with public health following the publication of the *Report on the Sanitary Conditions of the Labouring Population of Great Britain* and the *First Report of the Royal Commission on the State of the Large Towns and Populous Places*. The Irishman White was described by R. C. Gammage, the historian of the Chartist movement:

He was noted for his inflexible perseverance, and determination in everything which he undertook to perform, he was ever ready for whatever kind of work fell to his lot; whether it was to address a meeting, write a report, or collect a subscription, he was equally clever in each transaction. In battering the head of a policeman he was quite at home, and if circumstances had favoured, he would just as readily have headed an insurrection, quite regardless we believe, of the danger to himself. George's chief talent as a speaker lay in his ready wit and poignant sarcasms, which were launched forth in language anything but classical, and by no means agreeable to the polite circles though exceedingly well relished by men of a similar stamp to himself. George never did things by halves, but went the whole hog in everything which he undertook; and he never stooped to dissimulation. If he committed a wrong, he acknowledged the act, and defended it as frankly as though he had performed the most meritorious action. When accused by an opponent of having used unfair means to disparage him, he replied, 'Well, did not I tell you that I meant to put you down? and I have done it'. It is possible to charge George White with his almost utter want of courtesy; but his veriest enemy could never accuse him of anything approaching to cant, to which he always appeared an entire stranger.[19]

In 1839 Scoresby came to Bradford; to an Anglican Church which was in an appalling state. During the first half of the century, whilst the Nonconformist sects and the Methodists had rapidly increased their chapels and their adherents, the Church of England, like a great lumbering dinosaur, had done virtually nothing. Its church building programme had been pathetically small and it had allowed the initiative to pass to the Nonconformists.[20]

The church/chapel controversy was a dominating feature of Bradford's social and political life throughout most of the nineteenth century, and the period between 1839 and 1846 was one of acute controversy. To understand why religion was such a potent factor in Bradford politics it is important to remember that the Anglican Church was the Established Church of the country and therefore Nonconformists laboured under a series of disabilities because of their religion. There were restrictions on where they could be married or buried, they could not receive degrees at Oxford and Cambridge, and, most importantly, irrespective of their own commitments they had to pay for the upkeep of the church through Church Rates. For a man such as the Congregationalist Titus Salt this

state of affairs must have been particularly galling. Almost certainly a millionaire by the early to mid 1840s, he was treated as a second class citizen because of his religious convictions and like a common criminal when he refused to pay his Church Rates.

During much of the 1830s the religious divisions were kept under wraps as the vicar, Henry Heap, chose not to enforce Church hegemony. However, with the coming of Scoresby the situation was transformed. Scoresby was an ex-whaling captain from Whitby and he was determined to re-impose church discipline much as he would have enforced it on his ship. He walked into a series of major controversies and disputes about church rates and education and undoubtedly exacerbated the divisions with his book comparing mill conditions in Bradford with those in the model New England textile community of Lowell.[21]

It was this comparison and concern with the conditions of the workers which prompted the compilation of the Woolcombers' Report, while support and promotion of it by the vicar and his supporters was part of a strategy to wrest the political initiative and the moral high ground away from the Nonconformist factory owners. To some extent the leading Nonconformists recognised the danger of such an alliance and after the initial meeting a number of leading Nonconformist divines – including Jonathan Glyde, the minister at Horton Lane Congregational Chapel, and Benjamin Godwin of Sion Baptist Chapel, together with some of the leading Liberal manufacturers – got themselves coopted on to the Sanitary Committee.

The alliance of Tories and working men was a temporary one which collapsed as conditions worsened after 1845 and it became clear the Vicar and his supporters could do little to alleviate the sufferings of the combers. Faced by such a massive deterioration in their conditions, the woolcombers and their leaders turned to militant political action and insurrection which served to distance them from Tory and Anglican sympathizers who were unwilling to countenance illegal activities.

Although the Report failed to achieve its immediate objectives of improving the conditions of the combers, it remains a striking and powerful indictment of the sufferings of that first generation of workers. It was a report organised, conducted, compiled and produced by the workers themselves and outlined their condition in damning detail. In that, although it cannot compare with the great public health reports of the 1840s, it is a powerful adjunct to them.

The investigators who compiled the report visited some 324 houses which contained 2304 individuals and outlined the numbers of rooms these individuals had, the dimensions of the rooms, how many beds they possessed, how many were working in the house and the type of fuel used for heating the combs. They gave additional comments about the quality of the living conditions. The Report was structured to draw attention to features which could command middle class sympathy, so stress was laid on the paucity of beds and the numbers working within a domestic environment. This was intended to impress upon readers the combers' demand for their trade to be taken out of their houses and conducted in purpose-built workshops.

In overall terms it found that the number of persons per house was 7.11, and because of the paucity of rooms in the houses, most of which were two roomed, there were 3.88 persons per room. When it is borne in mind that the average dimensions of the rooms was 15 foot by 12 foot, then the scale of the overcrowding becomes apparent. It also found that there were on average 3.16 persons per bed. Within these overall figures there are some extreme examples of bad living conditions. In Thompsons' Buildings which was located close to Bradford Beck on present day Thornton Road, there were 95 persons living in 12 houses with more than 4 persons per room and more than 4 persons in each bed. In neighbouring Tetley Row there were 54 persons in 7 houses. In Grace Church Street in the White Abbey district there were 55 persons in 6 houses, in Regent Street 41 people in 3 houses and at the bottom of Manchester Road in Queen Street, 56 people in 7 houses.

The comments of the investigators add flesh to the dry statistics with their description of individual houses, localities and living conditions and their impact on the physical well-being and the moral condition of the inhabitants. In this they were drawing attention to a factor which could command the attention of the middle classes who were already disgusted by the moral state of Bradford. This was the reason for the investigators' emphasis on the small number of beds available to all the occupants, and in individual cases they point out the consequences. In one house in Thompsons' Buildings they stated 'a brother and sister worked together; only one apartment and one bed. She has now left in a state of pregnancy'.

For the largely Nonconformist mill owners there was an overwhelming fear that Bradford was a den of moral iniquity; that underneath the facade of improvement, symbolised in features such as the Chapel, Sunday School and Mechanics' Institute, there simmered a volcano of drunkenness, violence and sexual debauchery which threatened to engulf decent working men and women. That fear motivated the Moral Survey of 1849, commissioned by Titus Salt as Mayor in 1849.[22]

The relationship between morality and social conditions became clearer during this period and those with a more liberal attitude clearly recognised that a bad domestic and environmental situation underpinned the supposed lax morality. Bradford was disgusting and could compete with any of the other industrial communities of the period in terms of filth, dirt and disease. Essentially the problem was that the town had grown too rapidly in an era without the administrative structures to control and direct this rapid growth. Even at a later date when many of the lessons of the period had been assimilated, most communities could not have coped with such a rapid growth. The problems were legion. There was no sewerage or drainage system until the 1850s, so all the domestic and industrial effluent found its way into Bradford Beck. This steamed when it was released from the mill boilers, changed colour as different spent dyes were discharged, became clogged with the rubbish thrown into it and built up around the bridges periodically to flood the town with a liquid that was little more than raw sewage. The sewerage problem was compounded by the fact that the water from Bradford Beck was used to feed the Bradford Canal. Here, in a more stagnant form, it became the single worst environmental problem confronting the town. As the Town Clerk in the 1850s stated:

The Canal, in its upper reach extending into the town, is supplied with what can hardly be called water . . . and the almost stagnant pool so formed has been at times so charged with offensive gases as literally to have been set on fire, the flame flickering on the surface where the gas was bubbling out.[23]

It was little wonder that it was commonly known as 'River Stink'. During this period the whole of industry and domestic housing was powered and heated by coal. This in turn produced dreadful atmospheric pollution and, because of its position in a natural bowl, the town disappeared from view under a thick noxious and possibly toxic fog. However for some, reared on the tradition 'where there's muck there's brass', it provided proof of economic success:

Hail Bradford – in thy dark and smoky story
What though the mid-day sun in vain may shine,
Let smoke be still the index of thy story,
And soot in place of sunbeams still be thine.[24]

There was a range of other problems, such as the lack of graveyards. It was said that the Parish church yard was full in 1836, but little was done to rectify the problem and another 14,000 bodies had been interred there by 1850. The open slaughtering of animals continued in the centre of the town. At the heart of these problems was the fact that this was the first generation of people suddenly taken from a small town or rural environment and forced to live in an urban-industrial community. So rural habits were embraced with disastrous consequences. Many of the inhabitants tried to keep pigs as they had done previously and the town became famous for the size of its pig population. The vestiges of an earlier era continued, such as the Pig Market which was held on Bridge Street in the centre of Bradford until 1843. Those worst affected were the Irish, many of whom had come directly from the West of Ireland and whose experience in no way fitted them for Bradford. The greatest problem was housing. It was in short supply and that which existed was generally of very poor quality. The majority of houses constructed during the period were two roomed but they often had to cater for exceptionally large families. They were built without basic amenities such as a kitchen, a water supply and a toilet. Water was in short supply and commercial users always took precedence with the Water Company. The bulk of the population had to rely on the dubious water supplied by water carriers. Toilets were few and whole streets would share a privy whose waste would accumulate in a pile until large enough to tempt a local farmer to remove it. Every available space was utilised for housing and it is clear from the Report that large numbers inhabited cellar dwellings which were underground, lacked ventilation, were beset by damp, and in some cases flooded. It was little wonder that when the young German Georg Weerth came to Bradford in 1842, he compared his entrance into the town with a descent into hell and summed up the town with the words: 'that you had been lodged in no other place than with the Devil incarnate . . . if anyone wants to feel how a poor sinner is perhaps tormented in Purgatory, let him travel to Bradford'.[25]

The consequence of this fearful environment was widespread disease and death. During 1844 the public health statistics for the West Riding of Yorkshire showed the urban and class nature of death.

Average Age of Death in the West Riding of Yorkshire 1844 [26]

Average age of death in the West Riding	25 years 11 months
Average age of death in Ripon	36 years 3 months
Average age of death in Leeds	23 years 4 months
Average age of death in Bradford	20 years 3 months
Average age of death of gentry, professional persons and their families in the West Riding	39 years
Average age of death of agricultural labourers and their families in the West Riding	32 years 9 months
Average age of death of tradesmen and their families in the West Riding	23 years 2 months
Average age of death of woolcombers and their families in the West Riding	16 years

Deaths of Woolcombers in Bradford in 1844

	under 5	5–21	Above 21	Total	Average age at death
West Bradford	79	15	39	133	17 yrs
East Bradford	106	14	41	161	14 yrs 2mths

Underpinning the high death rate and low average age of death was an infant mortality rate so high that more than 50% of babies born in Bradford never reached the age of five. They were subjected to a range of diseases related to poor environmental conditions and malnourished bodies such as infant diarrhoea, fever, German measles, measles and scarlet fever. Against these there were few defences. The medical profession could offer little hope before the coming of such developments as antiseptic techniques and a wider knowledge of bacteriology and the transmission of diseases.

The other factor which could alleviate public health problems was the development of a local government structure able to confront the major environmental hazards. But in the 1840s there were many who were passionately opposed to the creation of a Town Council. Prior to 1847 Bradford was governed by organisations such as the Parish Vestry and the Improvement Commissioners which were incapable of responding to the social consequences of industrialization and urbanization. For the Liberal élite the answer was to develop a Town Council under the Municipal Corporations Act (1835) which allowed for the creation of an elected local assembly. But both the old Tory élite and the bulk of the working classes were opposed to this development which was effectively blocked until 1847. The reasons for Tory opposition were fairly clear. The Tories believed a Town Council would destroy the old Tory-dominated non-democratic agencies of local government, such as the Improvement Commissioners. But working-class opposition to, for example, sanitary reform seems less comprehensible, although there were a number of crucial reasons for hostility. The first was quite simply cost. Working men and women recognised that a Town Council would involve an increase in local taxation, a heavy burden for those already on the margins of existence. The second reason was the connection that was consistently made between governmental agencies and oppression. Throughout the nineteenth century there was a great fear of government intervention, whatever the avowed intentions. Working men and women regarded an increased role for government as a development that would further limit freedom and control working class behaviour. They had ample justification for their fears as the Liberal middle classes wanted a new effective local government system which would in turn introduce a police force. The police were detested amongst working-class communities, earning such epithets as 'the plague of blue locusts', because they were charged with enforcing rules, regulations and laws which seemed to be aimed at the pleasures of working-class life, such as drinking and gambling. In addition they were seen as an agency of political control, a powerful imperative in the age of Chartism. The third reason was that the middle classes wanted local government to clean up the environment and working class leaders had deep reservations about local government and sanitary reform. Direct environmental and public health intervention was consistently seen as falling most heavily on the working classes, with consequential losses in housing and increased costs. Also the poor environment was seen as being caused by the mill owners and the working classes believed that the mill owners should incur the cost of cleaning up their mess rather than passing it on to the community at large.[27]

After the failure of the Sanitary Report to achieve an improvement in the position of the woolcombers, their position declined dramatically. This decline and feeling of apparent hopelessness was best expressed by Abraham Wildman, resident of one the poorest streets in Bradford, Adelaide Street off Manchester Road:

The Lay of the Woolcomber

Wearied with labour, exhausted with toil,
A heartfull of sorrow, a brow without smile;
Oh! wretched condition,
Is this my position?

For long seems the day;
With bones aching weary,
With prospects all dreary,
I've scarcely sufficient to nourish my lay.

My cell dark, deep, is dug out of earth,
Where young ones around me ne'er gambol in
mirth;
In garments of sorrow
We beg, buy or borrow,
To clothe them some way;
Our fondest affection
Is cruel correction
To bar and to limit their innocent play.

The sweet breath of morning ne'er enters my
dwelling,
To clear the old fumes from the damp-colour'd
ceiling,
Which constantly oozing,
Keep soul-body dozing
In this dismal hole;
Whatever the weather
We're huddled together,
And breathe the slow poison arising from coal.

Six children and wife, with self, number eight;
A bed of deal shavings, our couch for the night;
We rise in the morning,
The same rags adorning,
To toil at the comb;
Like quarry-men digging,
We're snatching and jigging
One room is our workshop, our cookshop, and
home!

Alas, what instruction can render them civil?
Examples around them creating more evil!
A cheerless commotion
Flies far from devotion
And renders all vain;
The clothes on the Sunday
Are worn on the Monday,
Disease and dark poverty over us reign.

Come some one behold us with charity's meed
And see how the heart in its sorrows can bleed;
For comforts ne'er tasting,
Our bodies are wasting
By inches to death;

With cold shake and shiver,
Affection from liver
And gasping while working to draw the pure
breath.

Come rouse up, my young ones, half starved and
in blight;
The comb-pots our altar from morning to night;
Then stir up the fire,
More heat we require.
There's death in the fume;
Work, work, while you can,
Pale shreds of a man,
Thank God there's a rest and a peace in the Tomb

Although poor poetry, it captured the feelings of the woolcombers. Their heavy involvement with insurrectionary politics in 1848 lost them the sympathy of the middle classes. Individual attempts to help, such as the Emigration Aid Society, never garnered much public support, and certainly no financial assistance. From more than 10,000, the numbers of Bradford woolcombers rapidly dwindled so that by the time of the 1853/4 economic depression there were only about 2500, and as Samuel Kydd wrote: 'There is a certain uniform misery expressed in the face of the woolcomber. It is not melancholy, it is not grief; it is the sinking of the whole system – body and mind'. Their condition was appalling, as outlined by a local relief committee which submitted details to the Board of Guardians. Those details are given in full in the Appendix.

So where did this significant group of workers go? Some emigrated, in particular to Australia where the gold workings acted as a powerful bait. During the 1850s there are numerous letters from ex-woolcombers recounting their experiences of the harrowing journey to Australia and conditions in that country. Some were employed in the new employment structure after 1850. From about that point the trend which had seen the replacement of male hand labour by female factory labour slowed down and a range of male jobs opened up in areas such as the building trade, (which experienced a massive boom in the 1850s with the rebuilding of central Bradford); in the transport sector (which vastly expanded with the coming of the railway); in textile warehousing (which saw the biggest increase of any area of work in the 1850s); and in a range of other jobs which became available in the more settled economic conditions after 1850. The last time they were the centre of attention was in the 1857/8 depression when their numbers were very small. By that time they were slipping out of the public gaze, but they were a crucial feature in the development of the West Yorkshire worsted industry and their sufferings provide an important example of the human consequences of the new industrial system. Their fate shows that economic restructuring brought in its wake suffering and hardship and that the development of the Bradford Trade was not simply a catalogue of success but had its losers as well as winners. The lists of tables showing massive increases in raw materials imported, of finished goods exported, and the number of mill workers and those great grandiose monuments the mills themselves, masked a harsher reality of dislocation in the lives of thousands of Bradfordians and their families. As George White so eloquently summarised the situation:

> Is a man made in God's image worth less than a piece of stuff? Then go to Leeds Road end and see the palaces built to cloth.[29]

Bradford, of course, was not finished with woolcombing, for it was transferred into the mills and, significantly, it exhibited the worst conditions in the trade. By the 1890s the conditions of the machine woolcombers was the cause of much public comment and condemnation. In particular woolcombers who worked on nights, (and woolcombing was the only sector that worked nights in the trade), had to endure very poor working conditions. They worked a 64 hour week, often from 5.15 in the evening till 6 the next morning in temperatures in excess of 100 degrees without the benefit of breaks. Furthermore they were employed on a daily basis having to turn up each evening, often when it was clear there was no work for them. They were commonly known as 'Holden's Ghosts' after Isaac Holden, the owner of Alston Works, the biggest combing plant in Bradford. So the transition to a factory context produced few benefits for them – they remained a reserve army of labour as they had been in the 1840s and 1850s, when George White had stated that:

> ...Their trade was a sort of common reservoir of all the poverty of England and Ireland.[30]

References

1. *B(radford) O(bserver)*, 16 October 1845.
2. For the historical development of Bradford see James, J., *The History and Topography of Bradford*, (London, 1841); Scruton, W., *Bradford Fifty Years Ago*, (Bradford, 1897); Firth, G., *Bradford and the Industrial Revolution, an economic history 1760–1840*, (Halifax, 1990); Reynolds, J., *The Great Paternalist. Titus Salt and the Growth of Bradford*, (London, 1983).
3. James, J., *The History of Bradford and the Parish with Additions and Continuations to the Present Time*, (London, 1866), p.186.
4. For the best summary of the 'Standard of Living Debate' see Taylor, A.J., *The Standard of Living in Britain in the Industrial Revolution*, (London, 1975).
5. For a detailed analysis of the plight of the cotton hand weavers see Blythell, D., *The Handloom Weavers. A Study in the English Cotton Industry during the Industrial Revolution*, (London, 1969).
6. For the pre-industrial history of the Yorkshire woollen and worsted industries see Heaton, H., *The Yorkshire Woollen and Worsted Industries*, (Oxford, 1965).
7. Heaton, H., *op. cit.*, p297.
8. Hudson, P., 'Proto-Industrialisation: the case of the West Riding Wool Textile Industry in the 18th and early 19th Centuries', *History Workshop*, 12, 1981, pp.38–9.
9. Nicholson, J., *Miscellaneous Poems*, ed W.G. Hird, (London and Bradford, 1876), pp.263–4.
10. James, J., *A History of the Worsted Manufacture in England*, (London, 1857), p.250.
11. For the Worsted Acts see Heaton, H., *op. cit.*, pp.418–24.
12. For the 1825 Strike see Smith, J., 'The Strike of 1825', in D.G. Wright and J.A. Jowitt, *Victorian Bradford*, (Bradford, 1982), pp.63–81, and Myatt, P., 'The Rise of the Bradford Worsted Industry and the Great Conflict of 1825', *Speciale Vedhistorik Institut, Arhus University*, 1980.
13. Feather, G.A., *Oxenhope: A Pennine Worsted Community in the Mid-Nineteenth Century*, (The Haworth Society, 1972), p.29.
14. For the Irish in Bradford see Richardson, C., 'The Irish in Victorian Bradford', *Bradford Antiquary*, new series, part XLV, and Richardson, C., 'Irish Settlement in Mid-Nineteenth Century Bradford', *Yorkshire Bulletin of Economic and Social Research*, 20, 1968.
15. *B.O.*, 30 May 1861.
16. *B.O.*, 2 March 1854.
17. Engels, F., *The Condition of the Working Class in England*, (Granada ed., 1982), p.38.
18. See Wright, D.G., *The Chartist Risings in Bradford*, (Bradford, 1987).
19. Gammage, R.G., *History of the Chartist Movement 1837–1854*, (London, 1854, reprinting 1893, 1961), p.154.
20. For Scoresby see Scoresby-Jackson, R.E., *The Life of William Scoresby*, (London, 1861), and Stamp, T. and C., *William Scoresby, Arctic Scientist*, (Whitby, 1975).
21. Scoresby, W., *American Factories and their Female Operatives: With and Appeal on Behalf of the British Factory Population and Suggestions for the Improvement of their Condition*, (London, 1845).
22. *B.O.*, 7 March 1850.
23. Hudson, W., 'On the Public Health of Bradford', *Transactions of the National Association for the Promotion of Social Science*, 1859, (London, 1860), p.548.
24. Holroyd, A., *Collectanea Bradfordiana*, (Bradford, 1873), pp.139–140.
25. Weerth, G., *Samtliche Werke*, (Berlin, 1957) Vol. III, p.169, translation by Allan Farmer lodged in the Local Studies Section, Bradford Central Library.
26. *B.O.*, 28 August 1845.
27. For the arguments for and against incorporation see Elliott, A., 'The Establishment of Municipal Government in Bradford 1837–57', *University of Bradford PhD Thesis*, 1976.
28. *B.O.*, 19 June 1845.
29. *B.O.*, 6 November 1845.
30. *B.O.*, 10 April 1846.

REPORT

OF THE

BRADFORD SANATORY COMMITTEE

ADDRESS OF THE SANATORY COMMITTEE,

APPOINTED AT A

NUMEROUS MEETING OF WOOLCOMBERS,

Held at Peckover Walks, on Monday, May 5th, 1845.

The Committee having observed with unfeigned pleasure the exertions that are now being made by Government, as evidenced in the labours of the Royal Commission, to bring the deplorable condition of the Large Towns and Cities in this Kingdom before the attention of the public, in the hope of inducing all classes of society to take up this all-important and absorbing question. Considering that we are mutually bound to assist each other at this emergency, we have taken up our portion of the burden, and prepared a report of the condition of the Working Classes of this town: in order to induce the co-operation of all who can sympathize with the sufferings of their fellow-creatures; and also with the hope that working-men in other parts of the country may be influenced by our example.

We have upwards of Ten Thousand Woolcombers in this town and neighbourhood the major part of whom are compelled to make a workshop of their sleeping apartment; and as the nature of their occupation compels them to work over a charcoal fire, which is constantly burning in their apartment by day—and frequently left smouldering at night, in order to expedite the labours of the following day—the most dangerous and deadly vapours are thus diffused through the confined and ill-ventilated room, and continually inhaled by the inmates, who unfortunately have no property save their health, and no means of providing for their families when their bodily vigour is impaired and broken down by the ravages of disease. Sufficient proof of these facts are exhibited in the emaciated appearance of the victims of this awful state of things; uniformly followed by premature death. And numerous are the widows and orphans who are thus thrown upon the world, to share its sympathies, or sink under the sorrows which oppress them.

We feel deeply grateful to those who are now exerting themselves to remove this monstrous evil, and are disposed to give our hearty co-operation, in order to obtain for our families comfortable homes and healthy habitations; Our dwellings are improperly constructed, and totally inadequate for the uses to which they are now subjected, and as will be seen from the report, a most alarming state of physical and moral degradation is the inevitable result—our streets are filthy and in a most neglected condition—contagious and noxious vapours are hourly accumulating around us: even the common decencies of life appear to be disregarded; all of which circumstances might be avoided, if a proper system of sewerage and ventilation were adopted, and due attention paid to the other matters essential to health and common decency, wanting which we must ever remain exposed to attacks of fever and other contagious diseases.

The philanthropist can never engage in a more noble and praiseworthy undertaking. What can be more commendable than to befriend those whose labour hath contributed to make this great empire the most wealthy in the world? The moral condition of the people cannot be much improved, so long as the homes of the working-classes are so physically impure. Many of the vices of the age have their origin in the squalor and filth which surround the poor, and render them too familiar with scenes of drunkenness and crime, to remove which, we must elevate the character, and exalt the condition of the whole people. Let all unite and make this a labour of love. All may unite on this question, and the only distinction be, which can do most for society and for himself. Let us hope that the wealthy and the educated will co-operate with, and give efficiency to our labours on this occasion; and the heartfelt thanks of thousands will be their rich reward.

We are yours respectfully,

WM. DAWSON,	JOHN CARR,
GEORGE FLINN,	JOHN DEWHIRST, President,
JOHN HOWE,	THOMAS SPURR, Treasurer,

GEORGE WHITE, Secretary.

P.S.—Ministers of religion, Surgeons, Physicians, or other gentlemen, are respectfully requested to assist us by forwarding reports of their experience on this question—addressed to the Secretary, at the Committee Room.

Roebuck Inn, Bradford.

REPORT

OF THE

BRADFORD SANATORY COMMITTEE.

The Committee appointed to conduct this important enquiry, deem it desirable to state that they have carefully examined those parts more particularly occupied by the poorest portion of the inhabitants, and as it would require a cumbrous document to contain the full details of their research—they feel that they shall best arrive at the object contemplated, by selecting cases from various parts of the town, which shall convey a fair idea of the whole. At the same time the books shall be submitted to the inspection of all those who desire to satisfy themselves as to the real extent of the evils complained of. In addition, we beg leave to add that we have cautiously abstained from exaggeration, and confined ourselves strictly to plain unvarnished facts.

P.S.—For obvious reasons the commitee do not think proper to publish names.

RESIDENCE.	No. in Visitors book.	No. of Family.	No. of Apartments.	No. of beds in the house.	No. Working in the house.	No. of females.	Sort of Fuel used at work.	Dimensions of Apartments.				GENERAL REMARKS.
								ft.	in.	ft.	in.	
Cannon street	1	12	2	4	5	6	Coal	13	4 by	14	4	Dwelling situate in an entry or passage 2ft 10in. wide, bad drainage family in bad health, scarcely room to pass between the beds; five persons working, and twelve, including six females sleep in one room.
Do.	2	4	2	2	4	1	Do.....	14	11 ..	12	2	
Do. ...	3	4	2	2	3	2	Charcoal	12	9 ..	12	0	These three cases are nearly similar. Wife of No. 3 obliged to retire to rest in the presence of the man who works in the chamber. House enclosed on both sides by places for private purposes, which are exposed, and send forth a disagreeable odour.
Do.	4	3	1	1	3	2	Coal	12	9 ..	12	0	
Do.	5	4	1	1	3	0	Coke....	12	9 ..	12	0	
Do.	6	11	3	4	7	5	Coal	15	0 ..	11	9	The visitors give an appalling description of this dwelling, 6 persons work in the bed-room, 2 females sleep there—bad ventilation, no drainage, pig-stye and other nuisances.
Commercial st....	7	4	3	3	4	3	Do	15	0 ..	12	0	Extremely unhealthy—intolerable heat—3 men and a woman work in the bed room. An idea may be formed of No. 8, from the fact that two persons, father and son, were some time back, found dead in that place, from suffocation.
Do.	8	5	2	1	1	3	Coke....	15	2 ..	13	0	
Commercial st. frnt.	9	10	2	4	5	1	Coal	14	10 ..	13	2	There are two beds for the accommodation of four persons, in this chamber. Five persons work there.
Do.	10	10	2	3	5	3	Do.....	14	10 ..	13	2	These two cases are nearly similar,—deficiency of room for the number of inmates, bad ventilation, noxious smell in their sleeping apartment, 6 persons occupy 2 beds in the lower room of No. 11.
Do.	11	9	2	3	4	2	Do.....	14	10 ..	13	0	
Do.	12	10	2	3	5	4	Do.....	14	10 ..	13	0	Upper room used as a workshop for five, contains two beds for six persons, two of them females—obliged to deposit ashes in front of the door, through want of necessary accomodation.
Margerison's row..	13	5	2	2	4	1	Do.....	12	3 ..	11	2	No. 13.—This is a cellar, with two apartments, three feet below the surface,—bad drainage, continual stench, and the ashes suffered to accumulate in front of the door. An adult male resident suddenly expired in this cellar two months back: the coroner and jury expressed their astonishment at the existence of such unhealthy places, and pledged themselves to bring it before the public, but nothing has since been done to effect that object.
Do	14	8	2	2	2	4	Do.....	12	3 ..	11	2	Four persons work and sleep in the same apartment, which also serves as kitchen, &c. A child very bad with scurvy in its eyes. Bad drainnge, imperfect ventilation.

Flinn and Howe's Report

2

RESIDENCE.	No. in Visitors book.	No. of Family.	No. of Apartments.	No. of Beds in the house.	No. Working in the house.	No. of females.	Sort of Fuel used at Work.	Dimensions of Apartments.				GENERAL REMARKS.
								ft.	in.	ft.	in.	
Margerison's row ..	15	7	2	3	4	5	Coal ..	12	3 by	11	2	Same as No. 14. A female now lies ill in bed in a room where four persons work; the apartment is three feet below the surface.
Do.	16	13	2	4	6	7	Do. ..	12	3 ..	11	2	Six persons work, and eight, including two females sleep in one apartment. A large dam filled with stagnant water 6 yds. from the door.
Do.	17	6	2	2	4	3	Do. ..	12	3 ..	11	2	Same condition as the one already described.
Do.	18	11	2	4	5	5	Do. ..	12	3 ..	11	2	Five persons work and sleep in the back apartment. It is also used as a kitchen for eleven persons. Three feet below the surface. No drainage.
Do.	19	8	2	3	5	3	Do. ..	12	3 ..	11	6	Situation proportionately similar to the previous case.
Do.	20	10	2	4	5	3	Do. ..					Similar to the above. Six persons, including three females sleep in the lower apartment: five work and four sleep in the upper one.
Do.	21	8	2	4	5	3	Do. ..					Five persons work, and four, including two females sleep in one apartment—obliged to leave the window open through the night—one female ill in bed.
Do.	22	13	2	4	4	9	Do. ..					Four persons work, and five, including two females, sleep in one room—very hot, obliged to leave the window open at night.
Wappping	23	6	1	2	5	2	Charcoal	16	0 ..	11	3	This dwelling is four feet ten inches below the surface. No ventilation. Other circumstances like those already described. WAPPING.—This is an ill-paved, extremely filthy neighbourhood, the inhabitants are generally unhealthy and subject to malignant diseases. The cholera made dreadful ravages in this locality.
Do.	24	10	2	3	4	6	Do. ..	16	0 ..	15	4	Upper apartment used as a workshop for four persons, and a bed-room for six. Noxious vapours arising from the charcoal. Six females in the house. Bad ventilation.
Do.	25	7	2	2	3	2	Coal ..	15	0 ..	13	0	Similar to the previous one.
Do	26	4	2	2	4	1	Charcoal	14	0 ..	12	7	In this room four persons work over a charcoal fire, two persons sleep in the same. No ventilation—unhealthy stench.
Do.	27	7	2	2	3	1	Coal ..	14	0 ..	13	0	Three persons work and sleep in this apartment. Bad ventilation.
Do.	28	6	2	2	4	2	Do. ..	14	6 ..	13	0	Upper room very hot; four persons work and sleep in the apartment. The under apartment serves as bed-room for two and kitchen for six.
Do.	29	4	2	2	4	1	Do. ..	15	0 ..	13	0	
Do.	30	7	2	3	4	2	Do. ..	15	0 ..	13	0	The upper apartment is a workshop for four, and bed-room for six. Ill ventilated.
Do.	31	15	2	5	4	6	Do. ..	15	6 ..	15	0	Four persons work and eight sleep in the upper room. Lower room serves as a kitchen, &c. for family, and bed room for seven, including four females.
Do.	32	11	2	5	4	3	Do. ..	18	0 ..	15	6	Upper room, four persons work, and eight, including three females sleep. Three sleep in the lower apartment. Bad ventilation. entrance to the house in a narrow passage.
Do.	33	8	2	2	4	4	Do. ..	15	0 ..	14	6	Four persons work in the upper room; six persons sleep in the lower, including four females.
Undercliffe lane ..	34	9	2	3	4	3	Do. ..	15	0 ..	13	0	In the upper room four persons work, and five, including one female sleep. The lower room comprises kitchen and sleeping room for four others.
Do.	35	2	1	1	3	1	Charcoal	13	0 ..	12	9	Cellar—two persons work and sleep here. The fumes arising from charcoal very pernicious to their health.
Do.	36	5	2	2	4	2	Coal ..					
Wapping	37	6	2	2	4	4	Do. ..	15	0 ..	14	0	Upper apartment four persons work, and three including three females sleep.
Do.	38	4	1	1	4	0	Do. ..	14	6 ..	14	0	Cellar.—Four persons work, and three sleep in this apartment.
Do.	39	5	2	2	2	2	Charcoal					Upper room, two persons work, and five, including two females, sleep, near the pernicious vapours of charcoal. NEW LEEDS.—In addition to the other unfavourable circumstances detailed below, the smoke and sulphur arising from the Bowling Iron Works, add to the unhealthiness of this place.
New Leeds	40	3	2	2	4	1	Coal ..	12	0 ..	11	0	
Do.	41	5	2	2	3	4	Charcoal	15	0 ..	12	2	Three persons work, and three females sleep in the upper room, near a charcoal fire.
Do.	42	7	2	3	4	3	Coal ..	14	6 ..	12	4	Upper room, 4 work and 3 sleep. Bad drainage, ventilation deficient.
Do.	43	5	1	1	4	3	Charcoal	13	0 ..	12	0	A miserable cellar in which four persons work, and five, including three females sleep; four feet below the surface. Walls black with damp—stench intolerable.
Do.	44	4	2	1	4	1	Coal ..	13	6 ..	12	0	Four persons work and sleep in the upper apartment. A public necessary within 4 ft. of the door—stagnant water in the vicinity.
Do.	45	4	1	2	3	1	Charcoal	13	0 ..	12	0	Four persons, including three females sleep in this cellar; one man works at a charcoal fire.

Flinn and Howe's Report.

3

RESIDENCE.	No. in Visitors book.	No. of Family.	No. of Apartments.	No. of beds in the house.	No. Working in the house.	No. of females.	Sort of Fuel used at work.	Dimensions of Apartments.	GENERAL REMARKS.
Mill Bank........	1	9	1	2	2	1	Coke....	17 5 by 10 5	Mill Bank is situate in a low part of the town, behind the Sun Inn stables. It is filthy in the extreme—the street is narrow—drainage bad—stagnant water suffered to accumulate, and a most offensive smell continually emitted from the refuse which lies about in various directions. The figures on the left show that notwithstanding the foul atmosphere which exists in this locality, it is augmented to a fearful extent from the crowded state of the apartments in which the parties follow their occupations; and also increased by using cokes at their work, which emits a most noxious effluvia. It will likewise be seen from the five cases selected, that there are only seven beds for the accommodation of thirty-three individuals.
Do.	2	5	2	1	3	1	Do....	14 0 .. 12 10	
Do.	3	9	2	*1	3	2	Do......	15 8 .. 12 6	
St. Helena, Do. ..	4	8	2	2	2	0	Coal	....	
Do.	5	2	2	1	0	0	Do.	17 0 .. 15 0	
*Thompson's bdgs.	6	2	1	1	1	left.	Charcoal	17 0 .. 15 0	*In this case (No. 6) brother and sister worked together; only one apartment and one bed. She has now left in a state of pregnancy.
Do.	7	9	2	2	5	0	Coal	17 0 .. 15 0	Thompson's Buildings. Here are twelve cases taken by rotation, which will give a fair average of the condition of the inhabitants of that neighbourhood. This locality is situate on an eminence at the foot of which runs a filthy beck, or stream, impregnated with the refuse of dye-houses, manufactories, and dwellings contiguous to it. The streets are narrow and filthy, and the general arrangement of the dwellings unfavourable to health. The inhabitants uniformly complain of ill health. On reference to the figures it will be seen that these twelve dwellings are inhabited by ninety-five persons, having only twenty-three apartments for all purposes and twenty-four beds, making an average of four individuals to each bed, or eight to one bed-room, the average size of which is seventeen feet by fifteen.
Do.	8	9	2	2	4	0	Do......	17 0 .. 15 0	
Do.	9	6	2	2	4	0	Do......	18 0 .. 15 0	
Do.	10	10	2	2	5	0	Do......	18 0 .. 15 0	
Do.	11	7	2	1	4	0	Do......	18 0 .. 15 3	
Do.	12	11	3	2	5	1	Do......	18 0 .. 15 0	
Do.	13	8	2	2	2	1	Charcoal	15 0 .. 14 0	
Do.	14	12	2	3	4	2	Coals...	15 0 .. 14 0	
Do.	15	7	2	2	4	1	Do......	15 0 .. 14 0	
Do.	16	10	2	3	4	0	Do......	18 0 .. 14 0	
Do.	18	4	1	1	2	1	Do......	18 0 .. 15 0	
Lower West street, Tetley row.	19	2	1	2	4	1	Do......	13 0 .. 0 6	In those cases it will be seen that the inmates have but one apartment for all purposes—workshop, &c. It is therefore clear that the enjoyment of health is out of the question, especially as the street is narrow and filthy, and stagnant water suffered to accumulate.
	20	3	1	1	2	0	Charcoal	13 0 .. 6 0	
Do.	21	7	2	2	4	0	Coal	17 0 .. 14 0	Lower West Street, Tetley Row.—This locality is described by the visitors as being extremely filthy and ill ventilated, and the stench arising from the heat and crowded situation of their workshops or bed rooms as intolerable, resembling a stove room where sulphur is used. By referring to the figures it will be seen that fifty-five persons reside in five dwellings with eleven apartments, and only nine beds, being little less than six to each bed.
Do.	22	13	3	1	5	1	Do......	17 0 .. 14 0	
Do.	23	12	2	2	3	1	Do......	17 0 .. 14 0	
Do.	24	8	2	2	5	0	Do......	17 0 .. 14 0	
Upper West street, Tetley row.	25	11	2	2	6	0	Do......	17 0 .. 14 0	
Bottom of Victoria street.	26	6	2	2	5	3	Do......	14 0 .. 12 0	Five person work and three sleep in the upper room—very close—bad ventilation—heat intolerable.
Do.	27	4	1	1	2	2	Charcoal	12 0 .. 10 6	Here is one apartment at which two work at a charcoal fire, and four occupy the same as a bed-room—only one bed for all.
Do.	28	3	1	*1	2	1	....	....	***Bed in coal place—measured correctly, 3ft. wide—5ft. below the surface—three persons, including a female, sleep there.
Do.	29	3	1	2	2	2	Coke ...	12 0 .. 11 0	Working and sleeping apartment—very confined—noxious vapours from the Gas House cinders.
Do.	30	4	1	1	1	1	Charcoal	12 4 .. 11 6	Do. do. Unwholesome smell, partly arising from the use of charcoal, aided by the effluvia of a beck running close by the dwelling.
Do.	31	6	1	1	2	1	Do......	12 0 .. 11 0	Do. do. do.
Do.	32	10	2	3	4	4	Coal	16 0 .. 14 4	Do. do. Only three beds and two sleeping apartments for ten persons. Bad ventilation—great heat.
Do.	33	6	2	2	4	3	Do......	15 0 .. 11 0	Do. do. do.
Do.	34	6	2	2	6	2	Coal and Charcoal	13 5 .. 12 6	The whole of the cases in this neighbourhood are of the worst description; the streets are badly paved and ill drained, the apartments confined, and their inmates compelled to live in the midst of inconvenience and filth. No water except by purchase.
Do.	35	7	8	3	4	3	Coal	16 0 .. 16 0	
Do.	36	8	2	2	4	2	Do......	16 5 .. 15 0	
Black Abbey fold..	37	7	2	2	5	5	Do......	15 0 .. 11 4	Inmates in an unhealthy state. The smell arising from the place very unpleasant.
Do.	38	6	3	3	4	2	Do......	15 0 .. 13 6	Four, including two females, work here. Upper apartment contains two beds, two men sleep in one, and a married couple in the other.
Do.	39	7	2	2	4	3	Do......	18 0 .. 14 0	Very close, ventilation very deficient—disagreeable stench—obliged to take out the casement—general bad health.
White Abbey, Spink's buildings..	40	6	1	1	2	2	Do......	13 9 .. 12 0	4ft. below surface. In this miserable apartment, a man, his wife, and four children, sleep in one bed composed of shavings. General bad health.

Dawson and Dewhirst's Report.

4

RESIDENCE.	No. in Visitors book.	No. of Family.	No. of Apartments.	No. of beds in the house.	No. working in the house.	No. of females.	Sort of Fuel used at work.	Dimensions of Apartments.				GENERAL REMARKS.
								ft.	in.	ft.	in.	
White Abbey, Spink's buildings.	41	8	2	2	4	1	Coal....	16	0	12	0	No convenience for ashes or house refuse; inmates of an emaciated appearance. A fair sample of the effects produced by the system.
Do.	42	4	1	1	2	1	Charcoal	16	0	10	6	4ft. below surface. Four persons sleep in this apartment—ventilation bad—have suffered from ill health since they occupied it.
Do.	43	8	2	2	5	2	Coal....	16	6	11	0	Corresponds with the previous description.
Do.	44	10	2	2	5	4	Do.	16	6	11	0	In the upper room of this dwelling five persons work; in it are two beds composed of shavings, in which two males and three adult females sleep.
Do.	45	4	1	1	2	2	Do....	16	6	11	0	A pool of stagnant water opposite the door. One bed, in which two young men and their mother sleep. Apartment damp.
Do.	46	4	1	1	2	2	Cinders	10	6	11	0	A wretched habitation, very dark—a pernicious smell from the coke used in working—stagnant water opposite the door.
Do.	47	7	2	2	5	3	Coal....	16	6	11	0	No ventilation—very close—sulphureous smell—deadly heat.
High street, White Abbey.	48	2	1	1	3	1	Cinders .	15	3	13	4	A cellar six foot below the surface. This wretched cellar is a workshop for three, and a sleeping apartment for two ; foul vapours from gas cinders infest the place, and a pool of stagnant water near the door.
Do.	49	4	1	1	2	2	Coal....	14	8	11	8	This is also a filthy cellar, unfit for human habitation. Unhealthy in the extreme.
Spink's buildings, White Abbey.	50	4	1	1	2	2	Do. ..	16	0	10	8	Cellar—damp and low—no ventilation—four feet six inches below the surface—family in bad health.
Do.	51	10	2	4	5	3	Do. ..	16	0	15	0	Badly ventilated—family afflicted with asthma. The wife very ill—physician advises her to be removed from the town to recruit her health.
Salt Pie st. White Abbey.	52	11	2	3	3	6	Do. ..	16	6	14	0	Family in bad health—one confined to bed—three work, and five males and females sleep in the upper apartment.
Do.	53	5	1	1	2	3	Do. ..	15	6	12	5	A cellar six feet two below the surface—general bad health—stagnant water before the door.
Do.	54	8	2	3	4	1	Do. ..	15	4	12	5	Upper apartment used as a workshop for four, and bed room for five—very close—health generally bad.
High street, White Abbey.	55	8	2	2	4	3	Do. ..	15	6	13	6	Stagnant water near the door—upper apartment crowded with workers—very close and unhealthy.
Burner's fold, White Abbey.	56	5	2	1	1	3	Charcoal	15	0	10	6	This is a wretched dwelling—five persons lie in one bed on the floor of the upper apartment near the charcoal fire.
Wood street, White Abbey.	57	11	2	4	5	5	Coal	17	0	15	4	The extreme of filth and wretchedness—stagnant water near the dwelling—four persons work and sleep in a horrible hole seven feet below the surface. This case is beyond description.
Regent street, do..	58	4	1	1	3	2	Cinders .	12	6	11	6	A miserable cellar six feet two inches below the surface—filth and refuse mingled with stagnant water close to the door.
Do.	59	5	1	2	3	2	Charcoal.	15	6	13	6	Six feet below the surface similar to the above—very dark.
Do.	60	2	1	1	3	1	Do. ..	17	0	13	9	Cellar—no ventilation—general ill health—seven feet below surface.
Do.	61	9	2	3	4	4	Coal	17	0	15	6	Do. Do. general circumstances bad—two beds in the workshop.
Do.	62	3	1	1	2	2	Charcoal	15	6	13	7	A dark filthy cellar six feet three inches below the surface. In rainy weather it is frequently flooded as high as 20 inches ; a man with his wife and mother sleep on one bed in this wretched abode.
Do.	63	5	1	2	4	3	Coal	15	0	14	0	Upper apartment sulphureous heat arising from comb-pot—general bad health—a stagnant pool near the door—filthy street.
Do.	64	7	2	2	3	2	Charcoal.	15	0	9	6	This is described by the visitors as a horrible place. Continued smoke and stench in the house, which is surrounded by filth, refuse, and stagnant water.
Do.	65	7	2	2	3	2	Do. ..	17	0	9	8	From Nos. 65 to 69, it is truly horrifying. There are two privies within six feet of the dwellings, from whence the excrement overflows and sends forth an intolerable stench. Ashes, refuse, and filthy water accumulates with this and contributes to most disgusting scenes, truly disgraceful. |The dwellings near this vile place are thronged with human beings working and sleeping in crowded apartments. Mr. Booth, overseer of Manningham, has expressed his disgust at this locality. Various diseases have afflicted parties, from causes enumerated, especially in hot weather
Do.	66	8	3	3	4	0	Do. ..	17	0	15	6	
Do.	67	6	1	1	0	4	Charcoal	17	0	15	6	
Do.	68	6	1	1	6	0	Coal	15	0	15	0	
Golden sq., White Abbey.	69	11	2	4	7	2	Do. ..	17	0	15	0	The upper apartments in these dwellings are thronged with workers, and seven persons work and sleep in the first mentioned, who are continually inhaling the fumes of charcoal—drainage bad.
Regent street, Do..	70	11	2	3	3	6	Coal	17	0	11	9	

Dawson and Dewhirst's Report.

5

RESIDENCE.	No. in Visitors book.	No. of family.	No. of Apartments.	No. of Beds in the house.	No. working in the house.	No. of females.	Sort of Fuel used at work.	Dimensions of Apartments. (ft. in. / ft. in.)	GENERAL REMARKS.
Regent st., ditto.	71	0	2	4	4	3	Coal	17 0 by 9 0	
Do.	72	9	2	3	3	4	Charcoal	15 0 .. 15 0	No ventilation—a bad smell in the room.
Nicholson's houses ditto	73	8	2	3	4	4	Do....	16 0 .. 14 0	In the upper room which is very confined, four persons work and six sleep—bad smell in the room—family in a bad state of health.
Do.	74	7	2	3	4	3	Coal	16 6 .. 14 6	No ventilation—uniform bad health—two privies in the centre of a narrow street, the effluvia from which compels the inmates to close their windows in warm weather.
Providence street, White Abbey.	75	7	2	2	4	4	Do....	16 0 .. 13 3	Situated similarly to the previous case—this family removed from Otley, where they enjoyed good air, and consequent health.—Since they came to Bradford a daughter died of consumption.
Do.	76	7	2	3	4	2	Do....	18 0 .. 15 0	Privies opposite the door—no ventilation—a pernicious smell in the upper apartment.
Do.	77	9	2	2	5	3	Charcoal	18 0 .. 15 0	Ditto, ditto, ditto, ditto, ditto.
Grace Church st., White Abbey.	78	5	1	1	2	3	Cinders..	15 0 .. 13 4	Five feet below surface—no ventilation—inmates unhealthy—stagnant water before the door—smell intolerable—five persons work and sleep in the upper apartment, three of whom are females.
Do.	79	11	2	5	4	5	Charcoal and Coal.	19 0 .. 14 0	The inmates of this dwelling have an emaciated appearance—there are two charcoal pots in the upper apartment in which four persons work, and eight including four females sleep.
Do.	80	12	2	5	5	6	Coal	14 9 .. 3 12	The upper part of this dwelling is very small; in it five persons work, and nine including five females sleep.
Do.	81	10	2	3	4	5	Do....	18 0 .. 15 0	A dilapidated privy near the door, in which the parties who enter are exposed to the public gaze—upper apartment very close and disagreeable.
Do.	82	9	2	2	5	4	Do....	18 0 .. 15 0	This is a wretched abode, a sort of double cellar, four feet below the surface—flags in front of the door broken, stagnant water and filth springs up from the pressure of the foot.
Do.	83	7	1	1	2	4	Charcoal	14 8 .. 14 4	Five feet below the surface. Shameful! A mass of filth. A man his wife, and four children, together with his mother, lie in one bed in this wretched apartment.
New Leeds	84	7	2	3	4	2	Coal	16 6 .. 14 4	Upper apartment very low. No ventilation.
Pit Lane	85	9	2	3	4	3	Do....	15 4 . 13 9	Four persons work and six persons sleep in the upper room—family unhealthy.
Do.	86	8	2	2	4	3	Do....	14 7 .. 13 3	Four persons work and five sleep in the upper apartment.
Do.	87	9	4	4	4	4	Do....	16 4 .. 13 4	Upper apartment much crowded—four persons work and seven sleep there—family unhealthy.
Do.	88	10	2	3	3	6	Do....	17 0 .. 5 10	⎫ PITT LANE.—The chambers or workshops in this locality are very low and ill ventilated—they are uniformly crowded and unhealthy. Houses devoid of proper convenience. A drain from the mill gas works emits a nauseous effluvia.
Do.	89	11	2	4	3	5	Do....	Do.	
Rushforth's square, Barkerend.	90	3	1	1	2	2	Charcoal	15 0 .. 14 0	⎭
Do.	91	5	2	2	4	2	Coal	16 0 .. 13 11	⎫ These four cases are about the best met with; yet they complain of the closeness of their apartments and the unavoidable filth and annoyance arising from being compelled to work in their bed rooms—their health is generally bad.
Do.	92	8	2	3	3	4	Charcal..	16 0 .. 15 9	
Do.	93	7	2	2	4	3	Do....	15 5 .. 0 16	⎭
John Leah square, Silsbridge lane.	94	5	2	2	3	..	Coal	15 0 .. 13 6	Three persons work in the upper room, there are two beds in the same apartment.
Do.	95	7	2	2	4	3	Do....	15 0 .. 15 0	Occupied by a widow. Four persons work in the upper room. Five persons sleep there, including a female.
Middleton Field	96	4	2	1	2	2	Charcoal	12 0 .. 6 0	A double cellar extremely contracted—bed in a mere crevice near a charcoal fire—health bad.
Longcroft Place	97	4	1	1	2	1	Do....	14 0 .. 14 0	A cellar in which two persons work and sleep—they use charcoal.
Do.	98	6	2	2	2	1	Do....	Do.	In this case there are two persons working and four sleeping in the same apartment—two young women in one bed, and two young men in the other.
Do.	99	7	2	2	4	3	Coal	Do.	Upper room very hot from the comb pot—four work and six sleep there—general bad health.
Do.	100	7	2	1	5	3	Do....	15 0 .. 12 0	Very close—no ventilation—five persons work and two sleep in the upper apartment.
Do.	101	2	1	1	2	1	Charcoal	15 0 .. 10 6	A cellar six feet below surface—where two persons work and two sleep—stagnant water in front of the door.
Do.	102	4	1	1	2	1	Do....	12 0 .. 11 6	Similar to the foregoing.
Do.	103	3	1	1	2	1	Do....	10 0 .. 9 0	This family have resided here for three years, during which time they have been afflicted with uniform bad health.
Club Houses	104	7	2	1	5	1	Coal	17 0 .. 7 10	Ceiling very low—no ventilation—health bad.
Do.	105	10	2	3	3	6	Do....	17 3 .. 7 10	Ditto, Ditto, Ditto.

Dawson and Dewhirst's Report.   B

RESIDENCE.	No. in Visitors book.	No. of Family.	No. of Apartments.	No. of Beds in the house.	No. working in the House.	No. of females.	Sort of Fuel used at work.	Dimensions of Apartments. ft. in. ft. in.	GENERAL REMARKS.
Club Houses	106	9	2	2	5	1	Coal	16 0 by 15 0	Ceiling very low—no ventilation—health bad.
Do.	107	9	1	1	2	1	Cinders..	15 0 .. 15 0	Ceiling very low—no ventilation—health bad—very dark.
Do.	108	10	2	3	4	5	Coal	15 6 .. 15 0	
Do.									109.—Four persons work in the upper apartment, in which a man and his wife sleep. They had to cease from work a week since whilst the woman was lying in. She now lies in bed exposed to their gaze. A dead child is laid in the same room.*
	109	8	2	2	4	5	Do. ..	15 5 .. 14 0	
Do.	110	4	1	2	2	4	Coal	15 4 .. 14 4	A filthy cellar in which two men work. There are two beds in the same vile apartment, in which a number of men and women sleep indiscriminately. It is no better than a common brothel.
Do.	111	14	4	3	5	6	Do.	14 4 .. 13 6	Ditto, ditto, ditto, ditto.
Do.	112	3	1	1	1	2	Do......	14 0 .. 13 6	A pool of stagnant water near the door. Place dark and filthy. A man lies in the corner on a sack of chaff without covering.
Tate's yard, Market street.	113	4	2	1	2	3	Charcoal	13 0 .. 11 0	Upper room—two work and four sleep. This family came from Lincolnshire, where they enjoyed good health, but it has been the reverse during their residence here. Bradford Beck runs near the house.
Waterloo, Hall ings	114	8	2	3	3	3	Coal....	16 0 .. 10 7	Five persons, including two females, sleep in the upper room—three work there. The house is contiguous to Bradford Beck, which emits a most unhealthy smell.
Do.	115	9	2	3	3	1	Charcoal	16 0 .. 10 4	Five persons sleep and three work in a small upper room. The house is close by "The Beck." The house is in a yard thirty one feet by eight feet seven inches, in which are four coal holes, two privies, a pigstye, and an ash bin.
Do.	116	4	2	1	2	3	Coke....	17 0 .. 8 2	Four persons sleep and two work in this confined place. The stench from the coke is intolerable. The family have an emaciated appearance.
Back of the Ship Inn, Well st.	117	2	2	2	2	1	Do......	15 0 .. 8 4	A dark gloomy place—two persons work in the upper room. A young man and woman sleep there on separate beds.
Back of Market st.	118	4	2	2	1	2	Charcoal	17 0 .. 10 5	This dwelling is situate in a back yard, near Kirkgate. The entrance is in a passage twenty-seven inches wide, and fronting the Beck. It is a filthy, wretched place, unfit for a human dwelling.
Church Steps	119	8	2	2	2	4	Coal....	14 0 .. 10 7	Three persons sleep and two work in a very small chamber, entrance in a narrow passage. The church yard wall excludes both light and air from the house. Family in bad health.
Back lane, Westgte.	120	9	2	4	4	3	Do......	20 0 .. 11 0	Upper apartment, an attic, very low, in which four persons work and sleep. It is only five feet ten inches high.

*₊Such cases as these are of frequent occurrence, and ought to awaken the better feelings of those whose circumstances place them above such a revolting and humiliating position.

Dawson and Dewhirst's Report.

John st., Manchester road.	1	6	1	2	2	2	Coal ..	12 3 .. 12 0	Drainage perfectly stopt. Very damp.
Do.	2	5	1	2	1	3	Charcoal	15 8 .. 13 2	Main sewer stopt.
Do.	3	13	2	5	2	6	Do. ..	15 9 .. 13 2	Do.
Do.	4	4	1	1	2	3	Do. ..	15 10 .. 13 2	Do.
Do.	5	2	1	1	2	1·	Do. ..	15 7 .. 14 3	No.'s 5 and 6—Cellars, nearly six feet below the surface, drainage bad. Six persons work and sleep in these wretched places.
Do.	6	7	2	3	4	4	Coal ..	16 3 .. 14 11	Stagnant water within ten feet of the door.
Wm. Court, do	7	12	2	2	3	7	Do. ..	15 11 .. 15 3	A cellar, 4ft. 8in. below the surface. Two persons work there. Drain stopt—runs under the cellar floor—nauseous smell.
Newell's yard, do	8	3	2	1	2	1	Do. ..	13 0 .. 11 5	A cellar, 4ft. 8in. below the surface. Two persons work there. Drain stopt—runs under the cellar floor—nauseous smell.
Do.	9	9	2	2	5	6	Do. ..	17 0 .. 12 0	Three young men and two young women work in one room. Only two apartments for nine persons, male and female.
Do.	10	6	1	1	2	4	Charcoal	12 0 .. 11 0	A cellar 6ft. 6in. below the surface—two persons work in this place amidst the fumes of charcoal, and five sleep in the same apartment.
Do.	11	8	2	3	4	4	Coal ..	13 6 .. 13 3	amidst the fumes of charcoal, and five sleep in the same apartment.
Queen street, do	12	5	2	3	3	2	Do. ..	15 2 .. 12 10	QUEEN STREET.—One general description will suffice for this street and neighbourhood. It is a mass of filth—no drainage—
Do.	13	9	2	4	3	5	Do. ..	15 6 .. 13 4	the horse road unpaved, and nearly a foot deep in mud, together
Do.	14	8	2	3	5	3	Do. ..	15 4 .. 12 10	with stagnant water; houses generally crowded with men and
Do.	15	6	2	3	4	2	Do. ..	14 5 .. 13 3	

Spurr and Carr's Report.

7

RESIDENCE.	No. in Visitors book.	No. of Family.	No. of Apartments.	No. of Beds in the house.	No. Working in the house.	No. of females.	Sort of Fuel used at work.	Dimensions of Apartment.				GENERAL REMARKS.
								ft.	in.	ft.	in.	
Pinfold, Queen st, dc	16	6	2	3	4	2	Do. ..	14	5 ..	13	3	women working together indiscriminately. The back parts of the streets on both sides, have filthy yards and cellars, in which the inmates are also crowded together to a great extent. All this, added to the fumes of charcoal in several of the apartments, are calculated to generate disease. Several children have died of fever within the last few weeks, and a number of men and women are suffering from various complaints. An inspection of this part will convince the most sceptical of the necessity of establishing a comprehensive and efficient remedy.
Do.	17	8	2	2	4	5	Do. ..	13	10 ..	13	3	
Do.	18	6	1	0	0	3	Do. ..	15	5 ..	13	4	
Queen st., do.	19	5	2	1	4	1	Do.....	13	6 ..	13	3	
Do.	20	8	2	3	3	6	Charcoal	13	0 ..	13	0	
Do.	21	11	2	3	6	0	Do. Coal	13	0 ..	13	0	
Do.	22	12	2	3	6	0	Charcoal	13	0 ..	13	0	
Do.												
Duke street, do. ..	23	11	2	4	2	0	Do. ..	13	0 ..	13	0	DUKE STREET is rather better paved than the previous one, but on both sides are filthy yards, and the public necessaries shamefully filthy and neglected; a vast amount of wretchedness is to be found among the inhabitants. The remainder of the circumstances are similar to those in Queen street.
Do.	24	2	1	1	2	2	Do. ..	13	4 ..	13	3	
Do.	25	5	1	1	2	2	Coal ..	13	0 ..	13	0	
	26	12	2	1	3	0	Coal....	16	4 ..	13	4	This dwelling is situated in a filthy and wretched yard—in fact the whole of the yards between Duke Street and Victoria Street, are unfit for human dwellings. There are a number of filthy cellars there, which are chiefly occupied by woolcombers. Those places are dark and ill ventilated—wretched beyond conception. HOLGATE SQUARE is a miserable hole, surrounded by buildings on all sides. This place resembles a deep pit—no chance of ventilation; a number of men and women work in the cellars near charcoal fires. Seven feet below the surface.
Duke st. Manchester road.	27	6	0	0	4	0	Charcoal	15	0 ..	8	4	
Do.	28	10	2	1	4	0	Coal ..	14	10 ..	8	5	
Holgate square, do.	29	3	1	1	1	2	Charcoal	14	5 ..	10	4	
Do.	30	8	2	2	3	4	Charcoal	15	1 ..	15	0	
Do.	31	7	1	0	7	0	Coal ..	14	3 ..	12	6	Workshop in a filthy and confined yard—seven persons work in this space—there is not a free circulation of air—the yard enclosed on all sides.
Back Adelaide st. do.	32	5	1	1	1	2	Charcoal	14	3 ..	10	0	The visitors give a heart-rending description of this neighbourhood—extreme destitution and suffering appears to be the result of their crowded and unhealthy dwellings.
Do	33	4	1	1	1	1	Do.....	14	0 ..	13	0	Very damp—no ventilation—privy ten feet three inches from the door—three persons work and sleep in this filthy and confined cellar, five feet three inches below the surface.
Back Adelaide st. do.	34	5	1	1	3	1	Do.....	14	0 ..	9	9	Ditto, ditto, ditto, ditto.
Victoria st., do	35	6	0	0	0	0	Coal....	16	5 ..	7	2	Ditto, ditto, ditto, ditto.
Mary Gate, do.	36	8	2	3	3	0	Do. ..	16	7 ..	7	0	Similarly situated to the previous cases.
Do.	37	9	2	4	4	0	Coal....	16	7 ..	7	0	Ditto, ditto.
Do.	38	6	2	3	6	1	Charcoal	15	4 ..	3	3	Upper apartment contains three charcoal stoves, at which six persons work—there are two beds in the same room in which four persons sleep—bad smell—very hot.
Do.	39	2	1	1	2	1	Do. ..	15	4 ..	14	3	This miserable abode is situated over a privy—the stench is intolerable—only one apartment in which the inmates work and sleep.
Hope st., do	40	10	2	2	3	4	Coal....	14	3 ..	12	0	This is similar to the previous case.
Do. ...	41	7	2	3	4	2	Do. ..	15	10 ..	15	7	Privies and pigstyes in front of the door—ventilation bad—disagreeable smell.
												Ditto, ditto, ditto, ditto.
Nelson Court......	42	7	2	3	5	4	Do ..	15	4 ..	8	0	NELSON COURT.—A great many woolcombers reside in this Court. It is a perfect nuisance. There are a number of cellars in it utterly unfit for human dwellings. No drainage whatever. The visitors cannot find words to express their horror at the filth, stench, and misery which abounds in this locality, and were unable to bear the overpowering effluvia which emanates from a common sewer which runs from the Unitarian Chapel beneath the houses. Were this to be fully described the Committee might subject themselves to the charge of exaggeration. We trust that some of those in affluent circumstances, will visit these abodes of misery and disease.
Do.	43	8	3	3	5	3	Do	13	8 ..	12	3	
Do.	44	8	1	2	0	0	Do. ..	13	5 ..	10	11	
Do.	45	7	3	2	4	3	Do. ..	14	2 ..	12	7	
Do.	46	6	2	3	4	2	Do. ..	13	3 ..	10	10	
Do.	47	10	3	4	2	2	Do......	11	9 ..	10	0	
Do.	48	10	1	2	0	4	Do......	13	0 ..	10	0	Very unhealthy neighbourhood—a mass of filthy water within eight feet of the door.

Spurr and Carr's Report.

8

RESIDENCE.	No. in Visitors book.	No. of Family.	No. of Apartments.	No. of beds in the house.	No. Working in the house.	No of females.	Sort of Fuel used at Work.	Dimensions of Apartments. (ft. in. ft. in.)	GENERAL REMARKS.
Nelson Court	49	6	2	2	4	3	Coal	15 0 by 13 7	Ditto, very damp—a privy within seven feet of the door.
Union Street	50	4	2	2	2	2	Charcoal	15 0 .. 13 5	Family subject to disease, which they attribute to the filth and stench by which they are surrounded.
Do.	51	8	2	2	2	5	Coal	15 0 .. 13 10	A charcoal stove in the upper room at which three persons work—there are also three beds in which eight persons sleep.
Do.	52	14	2	5	3	9	Charcoal	15 3 .. 13 8	Four work, and three sleep in the upper aparment—very unhealthy.
Do.	53	11	2	3	4	4	Coal	15 3 .. 15 0	There are eleven wretched dwellings adjoining this, in which the inmates are literally crammed together in the midst of filth—no ventilation.
Do.	54	9	2	2	3	3	Charcoal	15 3 .. 15 0	Five work and sleep in the upper apartment—they say they are almost suffocated with heat. The place is surrounded with privies and pigstyes.
Threadneedle street	55	10	2	3	4	5	Do.	15 0 .. 13 3	Ditto, ditto, ditto, ditto,
Do.	56	6	2	2	2	3	Do.	12 3 .. 9 3	
Do.	57	5	2	1	3	1	Coal	15 3 .. 14 7	The mass of dwellings in this neighbourhood are ill constructed, the ventilation bad, and the inmates crowded together, working and sleeping in the upper apartments. The streets are ill paved, and stagnant pools abound in all directions. The inmates of those places complain of ill health, and attribute it to the above-mentioned circumstances.
Do.	58	4	2	2	3	2	Do.	15 0 .. 14 0	
Do.	59	7	2	2	3	3	Do.	15 0 .. 14 3	
Back do.	60	8	2	2	2	3	Charcoal	13 2 .. 9 0	
Do.	61	3	2	1	3	0	Coal	10 11 .. 10 1	
Vicar lane	62	9	2	3	4	3	Do.	15 2 .. 14 0	
Diamond street	63	5	2	2	3	2	Do.	15 0 .. 14 0	
Do.	64	8	2	2	2	4	Charcoal	14 11 .. 10 11	Very damp—no drainage. The tenant of this place complains of ill health, and was advised by Dr. Coates to leave the neighbourhood, but is obliged to remain not having the means of removing.
Do.	65	8	2	3	4	5	Coal	13 0 .. 12 0	Ditto, ditto, ditto, ditto.
Do.	66	5	2	1	2	3	Do.	14 0 .. 13 2	Four persons work and six sleep in two beds in the upper apartment. It is a wretched place.
Foundry street	67	9	2	3	4	4	Do.	15 0 .. 13 0	Very close and warm—disagreeable smell from the proximity of privies.
Do.	68	5	2	3	4	4	Charcoal	15 0 .. 13 4	Ditto, ditto, ditto, ditto.
George's court, do.	69	13	2	4	3	3	Coal	14 3 .. 13 0	Comb pot in the upper apartment at which three work. There are three beds in the same room in which nine persons sleep. part of them females. General bad health.
East brook lane	70	5	1	1	3	2	Charcoal	15 5 .. 10 5	A cellar four feet three inches below the surface of the street—very damp, &c.
Do.	71	6	1	2	1	3	Do.	17 3 .. 10 6	This is also a cellar two feet six inches below the surface—bad smell from charcoal.
Do.	72	3	1	1	2	1	Do.	13 9 .. 10 3	Very damp cellar—family in bad health—no drainage.
Do.	73	5	1	2	0	3	Do.	14 5 .. 13 11	Ditto, woman very ill. Dr. Stansfield advises her to remove in order to save her life. Too poor to do so.
Diamond street	74	8	1	2	3	5	Do.	12 6 .. 10 4	Ditto, sink close to the door—floor very damp.
George street	75	7	2	2	3	5	Do.	12 8 .. 10 7	Two charcoal pots in the small apartment—very hot. Privy close to the door.
Cartwrights' Yard, Bridge street	76	5	2	2	4	2	Do.	15 4 .. 14 5	Sink close to the door—drain stopt—the filth runs into the house.
Do.	77	7	2	3	1	5	Do.	15 4 .. 14 5	A close and unhealthy apartment—bad drainage.
Bridge st., Sugden's yard.	78	7	1	2	2	3	Do.	15 0 .. 10 0	This place is described as a perfect dungeon, unfit for a human habitation.
George's Court	79	9	2	3	4	5	Coal	15 5 .. 13 5	The inmates of these dwellings complain of ill health, and say they would gladly remove from them but cannot. The drains are stopt, and in some cases the filthy water from the sewers runs under the floor. The upper rooms are appropriated to workshop, bedroom, and kitchen for the whole.
Do.	80	6	2	3	4	1	Do.	15 0 .. 13 4	
East Brook lane	81	3	1	2	0	1	Do.	15 0 .. 9 8	
George street	82	7	2	2	3	2	Do.	....	
Do.	83	7	3	2	3	2	Charcoal	15 0 .. 10 3	Place very damp—unhealthy smell from charcoal—three persons work and four sleep in the upper room.
Do.	84	9	2	2	0	3	Do.	15 5 .. 13 4	Two charcoal stoves in the upper room—five work and three sleep there—disagreeable smell from the mohair which they comb.
Diamond st., George street.	85	11	2	4	8	8	Coal	15 0 .. 13 0	In the lower apartment five persons sleep in one bed—and three in a bed in the upper room where four work.
Frederick street	86	8	2	4	3	4	Do.	13 6 .. 11 3	Upper room very confined—no ventilation—five work there near a charcoal stove.
East Brook lane	87	9	2	2	4	5	Charcoal	15 0 .. 10 5	Place surrounded by privies and pigsties.
Do.	88	8	2	2	3	4	Coal	15 0 .. 10 5	Four work, and one sleep in the upper room.

Spurr and Carr's Report.

9

RESIDENCE.	No. in Visitors book.	No. of Family.	No. of Apartments.	No. of beds in the house.	No. Working in the house.	No. of females.	Sort of Fuel used at Work.	Dimensions of Apartments.	GENERAL REMARKS.
								ft. in. ft. in.	
East Brook lane...	89	5	2	2	4	1	Charcoal	15 0 by 10 5	Drainage very bad—a charcoal stove in the bed-room.
Cross street, George street..........	90	7	2	2	3	3	Coal....	15 0 .. 13 7	This family removed from Kendal where they enjoyed good health; they complain of ill health whilst living here.
Do.	91	9	2	3	3	4	Do......	14 9 .. 13 10	A privy within nine feet of the door. The walls are black with damp. Pigstyes close by.
East brook terrace	92	6	1	2	2	3	Charcoal	13 2 .. 12 10	This is a miserable cellar, in which six persons reside, and sleep near a charcoal stove. There are five cellars of the same description in the yard.
Do.	93	4	1	2	2	3	Do......	13 0 .. 12 5	Ditto, ditto. Family unhealthy.
Do.	94	5	2	2	3	2	Do....	13 0 .. 13 0	Three persons work and three sleep near a charcoal fire. It is very small, completely blocked up with a bedstead. The adjoining apartment is without window.
Do.	95	6	3	2	3	3	Do.	10 6 .. 7 3	Similar to the previous case.
Do.	96	8	2	2	1	6	Coke ..	11 8 .. 10 0	This is a vile place—six females and two males sleep in the midst of the suffocating vapour of coke: the mother is very ill, scarcely able to speak.
Do.	97	8	2	2	2	4	Charcoal	15 6 .. 14 6	A wretched abode—in the upper apartment two work and eight sleep near a charcoal stove. He has had five of his family ill at the same time, from the suffocating smell.
Ebenezer street....	98	5	2	2	3	3	Coal....	12 3 .. 10 0	A high wall in front of the door, also a pool of stagnant water—place very dark.
Do.	99	7	2	2	3	5	Do......	12 3 .. 7 7	There are thirteen cellars in this yard, totally unfit for human
Lower Globe fold ..	100	5	2	2	2	2	Do......	12 3 .. 7 7	habitation—very dark—no ventilation.
Do.	101	10	2	4	5	4	Do......	18 3 .. 15 0	Stagnant water in front of the door, together with ashes and night soil in large quantities—a disgusting scene. A boy ill in bed.
Do.	102	10	2	3	5	3	Do......	15 8 .. 15 5	Five persons work and seven sleep in the upper room—very much crowded—they complain of bad health—wife very ill.
Do.	103	10	2	3	4	3	Do......	16 8 .. 15 5	In the upper room of this dwelling are two beds near a charcoal stove—they are only eleven inches apart, and are occupied by two lodgers, a young man in the one, and an upgrown female in the other. Place extremely filthy.
Do.	104	5	2	0	4	3	Charcoal	16 9 .. 15 5	The upper room is very filthy—four persons work near a charcoal stove—several young children sleep in this unhealthy place.
Manchester road ..	105	7	2	2	3	2	Coal....	18 6 .. 10 6	Very dirty—no ventilation—bed in workshop.
Do.	106	7	2	2	4	1	Do......	15 10 .. 13 8	One bed in the upper room where four men work—ventilation bad.
Do.	107	5	2	1	2	4	Do....	13 8 .. 7 5	Two beds in the chamber, windows very small. Place dirty and unhealthful. Four persons work there.
Back lane, Westgate	108	6	2	2	3	2	Charcoal	15 3 .. 6 6	A low, dark, damp cellar, five feet four inches below the surface, in which there is one bed—family unhealthy—suffocating smell.
Do.	109	5	1	2	2	2	Do.	13 6 .. 13 4	These cellars are wretched places—the drainage is choked and
Do.	110	2	1	1	2	1	Do.	13 6 .. 12 7	emits an offensive stench. A woman is lying in at one of
Do.	111	4	1	1	3	1	Do.	13 7 .. 13 0	them and is in a deplorable condition—they are damp and dark, totally unfit for habitations.
Do.	112	8	2	4	5	1	Charcoal	13 7 .. 13 3	There are three beds in the upper room of this house, in which six persons sleep. 4 men and a woman work in the same apartment.
Do.	113	5	1	1	2	2	Do.	12 7 .. 13 4	In this residence, the enjoyment of health is out of the question, and little attention paid to morality or common decency.
Do.	114	4	1	1	2	3	Do.......	10 6 .. 13 2	In this cellar the husband works, and four persons sleep.
Do.	115	7	2	3	4	1	Coal....	15 0 .. 14 0	Upper room very dirty—in it are two beds. Four persons work in the same apartment.
Do.	116	7	2	3	4	1	Do......	15 0 .. 14 0	Four persons work in the upper room, in which there are two beds for five persons.
Do.	117	8	2	3	4	4	Do......	15 0 .. 14 0	Ditto, ditto, Three females and two males sleep in the upper room.
Do.	118	7	1	3	1	4	Charcoal.	18 0 .. 10 5	A separate chamber, at which a female works at a charcoal stove. It is also a sleeping apartment for seven persons, including three females.
Do.	119	13	2	4	0	6	....	....	This is a wretched dwelling—truly disgraceful—thirteen persons lie huddled together, on two bundles of straw on a damp floor, four of whom are females; the filth, misery, and tendency to immorality which such a condition is calculated to engender, is truly disgraceful.
Do.	120	13	2	6	4	5	Coal....	25 0 .. 11 8	Four persons work, and nine, including four females sleep in the upper apartment They complain of ill health.

Spurr and Carr's Report.

RESIDENCE.	No. in Visitors book.	No. of family.	No. of Apartments.	No. of Beds in the house.	No. working in the house.	No. of females.	Sort of Fuel used at work.	Dimensions of Apartments.		GENERAL REMARKS.
								ft. in.	ft. in.	
Leys	121	6	2	2	2	2	Coal	21 0	.. 11 8	LEYS.—This locality is well known to be the filthiest and most unhealthful part of Bradford. It is occupied by the poorest and most abandoned portion of the working classes. The visitors give a revolting description of the crowded state of the houses and sleeping apartments, and the mode in which both sexes lie huddled together, regardless of morality or decency. We have not space sufficient to describe this place. It is a perfect nuisance in every respect.
Do.	122	11	2	3	4	4	Coke....	14 8	.. 10 4	
Spurr & Carr's Report.										
Bowling	46	4	2	2	4	2	Coal	14 0	.. 13 6	* BOWLING.—This is a large and important district, situate on an eminence, having the extensive Iron Works in the immediate neighbourhood. The same general neglect of drainage, sewerage, &c., which has been already described, prevails here also; and is rendered worse by the close proximity of a large number of furnaces which continually send forth volumes of sulphureous smoke. All this added to the crowded state of the upper apartments and the noxious fumes of charcoal, tends to produce a state of things inimical to health, and destructive of domestic comfort. The four cases opposite these remarks are nearly similar. They are described as very close apartments; ventilation bad—inmates much annoyed by the fumes arising from charcoal.
Do.	47	7	2	3	4	2	Charcoal	....		
Do.	48	8	2	3	4	2	Coal	14 0	.. 13 6	
Do.	49	11	2	3	2	3	Charcoal	15 0	.. 12 0	
Ditto, Long row ...	50	4	2	2	3	2	Do....	15 0	.. 12 0	Four persons, including two females, work and sleep in the upper room, near a charcoal stove.
Do.	51	7	2	2	4	3	Coal		Do.	There are four persons who work in the upper room—three persons including two females, sleep in the same.
Do.	52	10	2	3	2	6	Do....	15 0	.. 12 0	Upper apartment very close—ventilation bad—four persons work, and six including four females sleep in the same room.
Do.	53	6	2	2	4	3	Charcoal	15 0	.. 12 0	Four persons work, and three, including two females, sleep in the upper room. A large heap of dirt, within three yards of the door.
Do.	54	12	2	2	5	6	Do....	15 0	.. 12 0	In the upper room six persons work, and nine, including four females, sleep. There are two charcoal stoves in the apartment. A suffocating smell is the result of this unnatural system.
Do.	55	11	2	4	5	5	Coal	15 0	.. 12 0	Five persons work, and eleven, including five females, sleep in the upper room—ventilation bad.
Bowling Long ro ..	56	9	2	3	7	2	Do....	15 0	.. 12 0	Seven persons work, and six sleep in the upper room—heat insufferable.
Do.	57	9	2	3	5	3	Do....	15 0	.. 12 0	Five persons work and sleep in the upper apartment.
Bottom of Bermondsey	58	12	2	4	4	5	Do....	14 0	.. 12 6	Six persons, including four females, sleep in the house; and six, including one female, in the upper room. Father and daughter lie in separate beds very ill.
School street	59	11	2	3	4	6	Do....	15 4	.. 14 0	In the upper apartment four persons work, and four, including three females, sleep—lower room ditto.
Mill street	60	7	1	2	3	5	Charcal..	15 4	.. 14 0	Upper room two persons work, and seven, including five females, sleep near a charcoal stove. House surrounded by filth—contents of privy exposed. A disgusting scene.
Do.	61	9	2	2	4	4	Coal	15 0	.. 14 6	House situate in a yard 51 ft. by 16 ft. In it are five other houses, three privies, a stable, and pigstye. In the upper apartment four persons work, and six, including three females, sleep. The other five similar.
Do.	62	5	2	2	4	2	Do....	15 0	.. 14 0	There is a stagnant pool close to the lower apartment, which serves as a Day-school for thirty children. No drainage.
North Wing	63	7	2	2	5	4	Do....	15 0	.. 11 6	Four persons work and two sleep in the upper room—offensive smell from the charcoal fire.
Do.	64	9	2	2	4	5	Do....	15 0	.. 11 6	Upper apartment serves as a workshop for three, and bed-room for four persons, includidg two females.
Do.	65	6	2	2	4	2	Do....	16 0	.. 14 4	Similar to the above.
Do.	66	5	2	2	4	1	Do....	16 0	.. 14 4	Ditto, ditto.

* Read the preceding cases attentively. Surely it is time to amend this awful state of things. These are taken from a neighbourhood comprising 54 houses. No drainage, nor receptacles for ashes. In some cases there are no privies. All this, added to the fumes of the Foundry, render this a most undesirable place of residence.

Flinn and Carr's Report.

11

RESIDENCE.	No. in Visitors book.	No. of Family.	No. of Apartments.	No. of Beds in the house.	No. working in the House.	No. of females.	Sort of Fuel used at work.	Dimensions of Apartments.				GENERAL REMARKS.
								ft.	in.	ft.	in.	
Bowling.........	67	9	2	4	4	4	Coal	16	6	by 14	4	In the upper apartment four persons work, and six, including two females, sleep.
Do.	68	12	2	3	4	5	Do. ..	16	6	.. 14	6	Ditto, ditto, ditto, three females sleep there.
Do.	69	8	2	2	4	2	Do....	12	4	.. 15	0	Four persons sleep in the lower apartment; four work and three sleep in the upper.
Do.	70	4	2	2	4	1	Do	12	0	.. 14	6	* This family are engaged in combing black Alpaca, which sends forth an unpleasant smell. The fibres fly about in all directions.
Do.	71	7	2	3	4	3	Do	14	0	.. 15	0	Four persons work in the upper room, and four, including two females, sleep there.
Do.	72	8	2	3	3	2	Charcoal		Do.			Four persons work and sleep near the vapours of a charcoal stove.
Do.	73	7	2	2	4	2	Do......	12	6	.. 13	5	Similarly situated to the previous case.
Do.	74	6	2	2	3	2	Coal			....		In this dwelling two females narrowly escaped suffocation from the charcoal vapour. A woman named Barber died some time since, from the same cause.
Do.	75	8	2	4	3	6	Charcoal	12	8	.. 18	0	Three persons work, and six, including five females, sleep in the upper apartment. One person laid in bed very ill.
Do.	76	5	1	1	2	3	Coal	13	0	.. 14	6	Two persons work, and five, including three females, sleep in the upper room near a charcoal stove. This place is occupied by a widow, whose husband was laid out in the room where the inmates worked.
Do.	77	5	2	3	4	2	Coal		Do.			Four persons work and three sleep in the upper room. No drainage—ventilation bad.
Do.	78	5	2	4	4	3	Coal ...		Do.			Similar to the above.
Do.	79	10	2	2	4	4	Charcoal	14	6	.. 14	10	Four persons work, and four, including two females, sleep in the upper room near a charcoal stove—very bad smell.
Do.	80	8	2	3	4	5	Coal	14	6	.. 14	2	In the upper room four persons work, and six, including four females sleep—room very close.
Do.	81	6	2	3	3	2	Coal		Do.			Three work and four sleep in the upper apartment. A filthy place—no ventilation.
Do.	82	8	2	3	3	2	Do......		Do.			The heat in the upper room is intolerable—three work and five sleep there.

* There are nine dwellings similar to this—they are situated in a yard, which, for filth and general bad circumstances can scarcely be exceeded. Some of the houses have no privies attached, nor any place for depositing house refuse. One man had to build a wall at his own expense to prevent the ashes from entering the door. The stench in this neighbourhood is very offensive.

Flinn and Dewhirst's Report.

THE committee, feeling deeply the great and paramount importance of the present enquiry, and being extremely anxious that a vigorous effort should *now* be made to remedy the grievances under which the working classes are compelled to suffer. Her Majesty's Government having felt the necessity of taking the initiative in this great work, voluminous Reports, emanating from the scientific, the wise, and benevolent, having been prepared and laid before the country, the thinking and humane must feel convinced that the time has arrived when *something effectual* and comprehensive shall be done. The co-operation of every friend of his species is urgently required, as an opportunity has occurred for removing the causes which lead to such a large amount of misery and disease. It has been clearly shown that malignant diseases, can, to a great extent, be removed, and health secured to all classes, in an infinitely larger degree than has previously existed. We therefore come before the public of Bradford with this report, trusting that the same ardent love of their fellows, may animate those who peruse it, as has been the guiding principle of the originators of the enquiry.

From the kindness and excellent feeling displayed towards us by clergymen of every denomination, and the wealthier classes generally, we have reason to feel a sanguine hope of the result of our labours. Our deputations have received a cordial reception; the most lively interest has been taken in the success of this great design, and from all sides promises of co-operation and support have been received. We have likewise been kindly favoured with communications from Sir Robert Peel, and the Duke of Buccleugh, as president of Her Majesty's Commission " for enquiry into the Health of Large Towns and Populous districts," and received from the latter nobleman, voluminous reports concerning the present question.

It appears by the report that the rate of mortality in Bradford is five percent greater than the average in all England —that medical aid is sought for to a great extent—that the heat and state of the air is most offensive and destructive of health, especially in the dwellings of the woolcombers, and that the streets and yards, occupied by this class of operatives, are infected with foul vapours, sufficient to disseminate disease and extend it to the other classes. We have embodied a num-

12

ber of striking and indisputable facts, setting forth the enormous amount of evil to which this state of things must inevitably lead ; and we are desirous of impressing on the public, the indispensible necessity of removing this glaring and undoubted auxiliary to the spread of the various epidemics with which this town has been afflicted. We have made copious extracts from the valuable reports alluded to, which are hereunto appended, from which it will be found that the objects contemplated by the committee, are entitled to the attention and support of all, and have no doubt it will be duly appreciated.

☞ We beg leave to direct particular attention to the " Table of Mortality for the West-Riding of York ;" a most valuable document, in which the real position of our population is clearly set forth.

EXTRACT FROM THE APPENDIX TO 2ND REPORT

OF THE COMMISSIONERS FOR ENQUIRING INTO THE

STATE OF LARGE TOWNS AND POPULOUS DISTRICTS,

(Presented to both Houses of Parliament, by Command of Her Majesty.)

REPORT of the CONDITION OF THE TOWN OF BRADFORD, by James Smith, Esq., of Deanston.

Houses, 7,246 ; Population, 132,164 ; Deaths, 2-4 per Cent; excess in number of Deaths in 1841, 696 ; Average age of Death, 20 years 3 months—of Adults, 50 years 7 months. Proportion of Deaths of Infants under 5 years, to total deaths, 29-6 per cent.

The town of Bradford is situate in an irregular valley in the West Riding of Yorkshire. A stream called Bradford Brook intersects the town, and, from the obstructions to the free flow of water in its natural channel, by the erection of Mill-dams and the encroachment of Houses, it frequently overflows the lower part of the town, causing much havoc in the cellars and lower floors of shops and dwellings. There is sufficient fall for the natural drainage if it was not so obstructed. The principal part of the town stands on a steep hill side running towards the east. The extent upon a level with the margin of the brook is long but narrow. On the West the town rises also upon a hill side of considerable steepness. The main streets are narrow and confined, and rise towards the summits on both sides. Some of the smaller cross streets are extremely steep, so that in many places the moisture fom the dungsteads of the upper houses drain into the cellars of the houses beneath.

In one street, where some houses of a better class have been built, the one rising above the other on the steep, the drainage of the upper houses falling in upon those below, causes constant ill health to the inhabitants, and fever is seldom absent from the locality. Near this locality, in a low cellar, I found a Woolcomber with his family. He told me he had formerly lived on the heights, in a dry situation, where he and his family enjoyed a fair share of good health, but since they came to live in the cellar, they had been visited with much sickness. He said he had come to that house for cheapness of rent ; and I was able to show him, by reckoning up all the loss of wages from the sickness of himself and family, which he detailed to me, that he was a loser to a greater amount than the whole rent of the healthy house he had formerly occupied. He said he saw the force of what I said, and declared he would look out for a house better situated. One beneficial effect of giving the people greater intelligence by a more complete and proper education, would be to enable them to appreciate the importance of placing themselves, as far as possible, in localities favourable to health. At the conclusion I shall endeavour to give, for all the population of the towns and districts in Yorkshire, such information as to the aggregate loss from preventive disease and death, as I did in communicating to this poor man.

The general state of the surface of the streets of Bradford is respectable, but in most of the inferior and cross streets, chiefly occupied by the working classes, the condition is quite otherwise. Few of those are paved at all; none of them properly. In some streets a piece of paving is laid half across the street, opposite one man's tenements, whilst his opposite neighbour contents himself with a slight covering of soft engine ashes, through which the native clay of the sub-soil is seen protruding, with unequal surface, and pools of slop water and filth are visible all over the surface. The dungheaps are found in several parts of the streets, and open privies are seen in many directions. Large swill-tubs are placed in various places by pig feeders, for collecting the refuse from the families, for which they pay in some cases from 1d. to 2d. per week.

The main sewerage of the town has been very defective, but some movement has been made of late in executing some sewers in better form in some of the principal streets. The chief sewerage (if sewerage it can be called) of the inferior streets and courts, is in open channels, and from the rough and unequal surface of the streets, the flow is tardy and the whole soil is saturated with sewerage water. The main sewers are discharged either into the brook, or into the terminus or basin of a canal which runs into the lower part of the town. The water of this basin is often so charged with decayed matter, that in hot weather, bubbles of sulphurated hydrogen are continually rising to the surface ; and so much is the

13

atmosphere loaded with that gas, that watch-cases and other materials of silver become black in the pockets of the work-men employed near the canal. The stench is sometimes very strong, and fevers prevail much all around. Taking the general condition of Bradford, I am obliged to pronounce it to be the most filthy town I visited; and I could see no symptoms of any improvement in the more recent arrangements for the abodes of the working classes. The scavenging of the streets is but indifferently done, and a depôt for receiving the scavenging of the streets and other filth has been established in the very rear of the Court House, where the authorities meet.

The chief slaughter-house is in the middle of the town, and forms a most decided nuisance to its immediate neigh-bourhood. The sewerage is defective, and the supply of water for cleansing most deficient.

The supply of water for the inhabitants is very limited; but an act has just been obtained by a Joint Stock com pany for procuring a better supply, At present a great part of the town is supplied by water-carriers, who bring the water upon Carts or donkeys, and charge a half-penny for three gallons, which is most expensive, especially to the poor inhabit-ants, and forces an economy in the use of this most important element, highly injurious to health, cleanliness and comfort.

The woolcombing is admitted to be a very unhealthy employment. The woolcombers assort the wool chiefly in an apartment of their own dwelling. The work is done over a fire of charcoal, which sends forth volumes of carbonic acid gas and the workpeople are obliged to keep the windows open in all weathers to prevent, or mitigate, the evil effects of the gas. They are roasted to perspiration on one side, and have often a current of cold air rushing upon them from the window. They look pale and cadaverous, and are shot lived, few reaching fifty years of age. Their roasting employment and exposure to the carbonic acid gas, gives them a desire for spirits and opiates, and it is probable that the frequent free use of them may have some considerable share in shortening their lives. In some instances, where they have been brought to work together in factories, their health has been improved, and their habits have become better regulated.

The following is extracted from Mr. Clough's Report—page 338.

" The Bradford Beck passes through the most populous parts of the town. The stream, as stated above, is the re-ceptacle for the filth of the town, and during the dry season of the year emits very offensive smells. It is liable to swell-in rainy weather, and the lower part of the town is inundated. These inundations of late years have become more frequent in consequence of the encroachments made by building, either in or over the watercourse, which prevent the ready flow of the water. The owners of the property on either side, measure and sell half the bed of the stream, and the purchaser, as a matter of course, thinks he has a right to appropriate this as he thinks fit. During last summer the surveyors were de-sirous of removing a deposit which had accumulated under one of the bridges, the removal of which would assist the escape of the water, and greatly tend to prevent a recurrence of floods; but they were advised that they had no power to interfere in any part of the stream. They are of opinion that they ought to have power to prevent any further encroachments in the bed of the beck: and also to have the power to lower all or any part of the bed; and to flag or pave it if they think proper; so that the water, in times of flood, may escape the more rapidly. It ought to be stated that the registrars after a flood, notice an increase of deaths from epidemic disorders in those parts of the town which have been flooded.

Extracted from Answers to Queries of Commissioners, by G. R. Mossman, Esq., Clerk to the Justices for the Eastern division of Morley, and to the Lighting and Watching Commissioners.—Appendix p. 335.

Question 8.—Have the houses proper necessaries? Are they so arranged as to empty into drains, or into cess-pools, or in what manner are they cleansed? Are there any public necessaries; and if so, in what state are they kept, and under what regulations?

Answer.—Few cottages have proper necessaries; they are either too near or built with an open ashplace, and so in either way offensive; in some instances, almost draining into the dwellings. The necessary dirt is in almost every instance carted away. No public necessaries, but frequently one necessary for several dwellings in a yard. *(Cul de sac.)*

Question 9.—Are the house drains properly cleansed by water or other means, or does the refuse accumulate in them so that they become choked and emit offensive smells?

Answer.—The house drains very frequently emit offensive smells.

Question 17.—Are the houses provided with dust-bins for the reception of refuse, and how frequently, and in what mode are they cleansed?

Answer.—A negative reply ———　　*　　*　　*　　*　　*　　*　　*

Extract from General Observations. By James Smith, Esq., of Deanston.—Appendix to 2nd Report, p. 319.

" By the poor people, when the nature of our inquiry was understood, it was everywhere well received, But a lour-ing front was occasionally met with on the part of persons in a condition of life where it might not be expected; sometimes an aspect was exhibited of disapproval of interference " with local self government," and intrusion; and allegations were

14

heard that the people disliked to be interfered with, and liked dirt, and would not have their habits disturbed. Every such manifestation turned out to be from the possessor or sharer of one of those immense catch pits, or some pestilential interest or other, which a complete system of cleansing and purification would apparently disturb.

In the perambulation of the lower districts, inhabited by the poorer classes, it was often very affecting to see how resolutely they strove for decency and cleanliness amidst the adverse circumstances; to see the floors of their houses and the steps washed clean, made white with the hearthstone, when the first persons coming into the house must spoil their labours, with the mud from the street kept filthy by neglect of proper scavenging; to see their clothes washed and hung out to dry, but befouled by soot from the neighbouring furnaces; and to see their children attempted to be kept clean, but made dirty from the like causes; and sometimes to see those children, notwithstanding all their care, pale, sickly, and drooping, evidently from the pestilential miasma, of a natural stream converted into a sewer, and dammed up for the sake of mill power, in the hands of persons of great influence in the return of Members to the Town Council, who are deaf to all statements of evidence of the evil, or of the possibility of amendment.   *   *   *   *   *

In many instances either cellar dwellings having their floors from four to seven feet under the level of the surface, or dwellings having their first floors under the level of the ground, or just level with it, are the chief residences of the lower grades of the working classes.

The depots for the ashes and filth of the families are generally immediately adjoining the dwellings, open to view, frequently covering large spaces of the Courts or Streets, and with privies attached, exposed in defiance of all feelings of decency; and in all most offensive to sight, and to smell, and constantly emitting effluvia hurtful to health. The people in general are most sensible of the evils, and make every effort to induce the proprietors to have the nuisance removed or abated, but seldom succeed. The dung is in few instances removed oftener then once in six months, and then an extensive surface exhaling offensive effluvia from the saturated ground is left exposed.

There is want of a well regulated system for the scavenging or otherwise cleansing the alleys and courts, and in general a want of power to have cleanliness enforced, and nuisances removed from private courts and premises.

The want of sufficient and constant supplies of water at high pressure for ordinary domestic purposes, and for more thorough cleansing.

A want of sufficient lighting by gas in the Alleys and Courts.

There is a great want of width and openness in the Streets, Alleys; and Courts, especially in those parts inhabited by the working classes. Houses are built without means of ventilation sufficient for the number of individuals generally living in each apartment.

As a further elucidation of the remedy for the deplorable state of things enumerated in the report, we submit the following interesting extract from a well-conducted and talented periodical.

DWELLINGS FOR WORKPEOPLE.

At the new port of Birkenhead, which is rising up to be a great town before our eyes, a practical experiment is in progress, highly interesting to the working classes. The town is planned on a liberal and foreseeing view, so as to avoid the sources of discomfort and ill-health which affect those cities that grow up by hap-hazard; with well arranged streets, public grounds, and a complete system of drainage. To the place have been brought large flocks of workpeople for whom it has been necessary to provide dwelling; and in doing this for their work people, the Birkenhead Dock Company have seized the opportunity of dealing with the matter in so complete a way as to make a model for others to follow. They have taken into account the cost, the profit to the owner, the comfort of the inmates, and the general comfort of their neighbours. They have found it a better economy to build large houses rather than cottages; the have adopted a plan prepared by Mr. Charles Evans Lang, of London; and the buildings are now in progress. The ground which they are to occupy lies between two of eight streets that meet in a circus, and may be described as a triangle; across which, from street to street houses are erected in rows, with alleys between them; there is a school house at the apex of the triangle, and in the centre of the circus is a handsome church. Each row resembles what in Scotland is called a "land,"—a pile four stories high, comprising several distinct houses, each house having a public staircase communicating with the several "flats" or stories; each flat divided into two separate dwelling places. Each dwelling contains a "living-room," two bed-roooms, and a "yard." The living-room is capacious and well arranged for ventilation and comfort; on the one side are the entrance door and the door into the yard; on the next side, near to the entrance, are the doors into the two bed-rooms; on the third side, opposite to the bed-room doors, is the window; and on the fourth side is the fire-place: nearly half of the room towards this fourth side, is left without any door or opening, so that the hearth is removed from direct draughts. In this room there is a gas pipe, for light. The yard is a sort of scullery, but comprising the sink, coal-hole, dust hole, &c.: in short, all the "domestic offices," packed into a very close space, but fitted with conveniences not always found even in the houses of the middle classes. Up the whole height of the building is a shaft, with which the pipes from each yard communicate; at the top is a cistern with a preparation for keeping it full, to the extent of one thousand gallons of water; from which, independently of individual use, a stream can at pleasure be made to rush down the shaft, carrying away the *ejicienda* into the sewer, into which the shaft runs below. There is in that respect the most complete means for securing tidiness, decency

15

and health. The independent run of water will be a guard against many of the evils even of individual negligence; but it is inconceivable that with such conveniences the humble tenants should not acquire the better habits that await an opportunity. At the top of the building is an "airing flat," in which all the families whose dwellings open into the common staircase will have the right to dry their clothes. There is, we believe, some means of regulating the temperature of the whole pile of the buildings; at all events there are appliances to secure thorough ventilation; and the whole structure is fire-proof. The external aspect of these dwellings for the poor is handsome, and even imposing; in a style so ornate as quite to relieve them from the aspect of alms-houses; to which, indeed they bear no sort of resemblance. Now, it is calculated that this kind of house-property will "pay," even as a commercial speculation; with all this convenience and salubrity to the tenant, and let to him at the rent he usually pays,—the landlord, too, settling all rates and other charges, so that the tenant will pay for the whole house, its, gas-light, water, taxes, rates, and all, one fixed weekly charge,—with all these unwonted comforts and facilities, the tenant paying no more rent than he has used to pay for bad lodgings elsewhere, the landlord will yet reap a profit of from 8 to 10 per cent on the capital invested. In the present instance that is not the whole advantage derived by the landlords, the Company; for they will find great immediate convenience from the concentration of their workpeople, and great benefit may be expected by all who have a stake in the town, from the improved salubrity and the. high character which these far-seeing plans must secure for it. The experiment may prove to the speculative builder, that he could provide for the humbler classes, a very superior kind of accommodation at a profit to himself; it may also teach those classes what they should obtain for their money.—*Spectator.*"

The committee in presenting the foregoing sketch, feel it necessary to remind the reader that as their means were limited and precarious, they have felt great diffidence as to the extent to which their investigations could be consistently carried. Several highly influential gentlemen expressed a desire that the report should embrace a more searching and comprehensive enquiry into the various causes which produce disease, whilst others seemed to deem such to be non-essential to the object contemplated. We therefore resolved to give a condensed statement of facts, selected with great care, and in such a manner as to convey a fair idea and correct picture of the actual and unexaggerated position of the working classes of this town.

It may appear to some that the enquiry is too limited, and too much confined to a certain class of workpeople; but to this it may be replied—that the cases enumerated prove, beyond the possibility of doubt, that the benefits of the proposed governmental plan cannot possibly be enjoyed by this town, unless the grievances which are so clearly enumerated are effectually removed. It is not the working classes alone who are injured by the present deplorable state of things, for all must suffer in proportion to the magnitude or extent of the physical and moral evils which exist; and, by referring to the facts contained in the report—on examination of the facilities which exist for encouraging and strengthening evil propensities, and the obstacles which are placed in the way of that improvement which might reasonably be expected to result from the rapid strides with which this great and powerful nation have advanced in arts, sciences, and manufactures, and the general means of developing the mighty resources of this, the wealthiest country in the world; it is therefore hoped that all who are possessed of humane and discriminating minds, will see the necessity of establishing a totally different system to that which now obtains, and of surrounding the working classes with those primary circumstances which create self respect, and tends to exalt the character of the whole people. For the formation of which, it is needless to say, that good air, commodious apartments, and general habits of cleanliness, form indispensible ingredients. In relation to this subject, we cannot do better than give a remark from the report of J. B. Martin, Esq., selected from page 298 of the appendix to 2nd Report, previously alluded to.

"Whilst men are in the lowest state of physical destitution, surrounded by filth, vermin, privation, and squalor of every kind, familiar with sickness and death, and strangers to every comfort, with the mind continually on the rack, or absorbed in striving against physical necessities, or with the animal spirits broken down by its pressure; how is it to be expected that obedience to the laws, and that morals, education, or religion, should find a place? How can a man whose mind is ruined even more effectually than his body—the man by whom moral degradation and physical suffering have done their worst—how can such a man be expected to give a passing thought even to such matters? The thing is impossible. But not to speak of those higher considerations, I should say, that the benefits of the surrounding civilization even, are not for the occupants of the lanes, courts, and alleys through which I have of late passed."

Here is a vivid but true picture of the general condition of those in whose behalf we appear before the public. It is fervently hoped by the committee, that the excellent suggestions of the wise, benevolent, and scientific gentlemen who have originated this all-important enquiry, may not be marred by listlessness or neglect. We have no hesitation in asserting that in no town in England of a similar extent, is there to be found a greater amount of physical and moral degradation, than in this: so much so, that some of the *facts* contained in our Report seem to surpass belief, but we are fully prepared to substantiate them all.

To such as reside in Bradford, it will be needless to set forth the inefficiency of the existing cottages for the purposes to which they are generally appropriated; disease and immorality must be the inevitable consequence of crowding as many as ten persons into a small and ill-contrived room, scarcely sufficient for the necessary accommodation of two persons. This is rendered considerably worse by the same rooms being converted into workshops of a most unhealthy

16

description; where in many instances, the inmates of all ages and both sexes, are doomed to breath the pestilential vapours of charcoal, or gas-house cinders, both of which are extremely detrimental to health. This cause should, in itself, have sufficient weight with all who are interested in the temporal welfare of their fellow-creatures. But there are other and higher grounds, which (on perusal of the Report) must force itself on the attention of all, save those whose hearts are steeled against the dictates of religion and morality; we allude to the indiscriminate manner in which the sexes are crowded together in the sleeping apartments. Few, unacquainted with the true condition of the working classes, can imagine the unfavourable and revolting position in which they are placed, especially in this respect. Many are the bitter pangs and unavailing regrets which affect those whose necessities compel them to outrage the finest and holiest feelings of the human heart. Let it not be imputed to the working classes that this state of things is of their own creation—caused by their own improvidence and neglect. Far-seeing and intelligent men can plainly distinguish between the innocent victim of an unnatural system, and those, who possessing facilities for cleanliness, comfort, and a due observance of those social obligations which should impel them to preserve the morals of the rising generation from contamination—wilfully neglect them. Let us hope that better and more charitable feelings will animate those, who, from their position in society, are enabled to hold out a helping hand to their less fortunate brethren; and that on this vital question, the prejudices and estrangements which have heretofore existed may be extinguished, and give place to an expansive benevolence; and that some earnest shall now be given, that although separated by circumstances, we may unite in one great effort to work out a practical good.

In addition to the cirumstances already adverted to, it is necessary to point out the evil consequences arising from bad drainage, imperfect or neglected sewerage, and want of proper receptacles for the usual refuge of dwellings. We have selected extracts from reports forwarded to the "Health of Towns Commission" which will bear out the evidence collected by the members of our Committee:—Few towns are worse circumstanced, even in that respect, than this, and we feel that a regard to the health of the town generally, independent of the other considerations, ought to be an inducement sufficiently strong to impel the active co-operation of all.

Having entered thus far into the peculiar grievances complained of, we trust it will not be deemed presumptive on our parts to lay down a few ideas as to the *remedy*, which has suggested itself to our minds. We do so, not through dogmatism or vanity, but feel that some who peruse these observations may remark "Well, I have read through the report, I admit the existence of the evils, but what remedy is proposed by those who suffer from them?"

We are aware that this is a portion of the general question which requires deep thought—that it should not be brought forward in a crude or undigested state, but we also feel that the public will require some suggestions from this committee as to what remedy they would propose. At the same time that we do so, we wish it to be perfectly understood that we shall gladly avail ourselves of any improvement that may be hereafter introduced.

Through the same feeling which has guided us throughout this inquiry, we think it preferable to give an extract which may tend to place our views and wishes more prominently before the wealthier classes, and we shall feel extremely grateful to those who will enter into the same spirit as the gentleman to whom the following refers:—

MR. CUBITT'S WORKSHOPS.

" Mr. Cubitt's establishment offers many objects of great interest for consideration, and it is of these we propose to speak briefly in the present article. A minute description of it, shewing its extent, comprehensiveness, and completeness—the modes of economising labour, and the new processes employed, would be equally instructive and interesting. As, however, this would excite curiosity, and lead to applications which the proprietor would be compelled to refuse on account of the interruption they would cause, we would speak rather of the results, and the motives which are seen to prevail, than of themselves.

" Amongst the most important of the latter, apparent at every step, is a desire to raise the condition of his workmen; a desire so wise and so good, that we cannot praise it loudly enough, or set it forth for imitation too forcibly. The men literally work in drawing-rooms, large and lofty (the carpenter's shop is about 200 feet long), equally heated and well ventilated. Attached to each shop is an apartment for cooking, with oven, boiler, and hot-plate, where they may dress their dinner or prepare their tea. And here, high up under the roof, are rails, where they may dry their coats after a wet walk to their work. In order to prevent the men, as far as possible, from acquiring the habit of drinking spirits in the morning, they may have a cup of hot coffee or cocoa, by arrangement amongst themselves, on payment of *one half-penny* ! The consumption being large and certain, one half-penny pays the expense of a cup of coffee, a fact that speaks volumes, and points the way for an amazing increase of the personal comforts of the operative classes. Hot water is used to heat the shops, and the range of water closets belonging to each department is ventilated by superfluous warm air.

"In the smith's shop, in the mason's shop—one usually so smoky, the other so wet—all is clean, dry, and warm, and here, as the shops themselves are hardly suited for eating in, there is a dining-room, with table and benches connected with the cooking apparatus. When to all this we add that there is a lending library, comprising some of the best scientific and elementary books, and a room supplied with the daily papers to which the foremen have access at particular hours, it will be seen how much the comfort of the men is studied.

The result, it is gratifying to know, is exactly what might be expected. The best workmen are anxious to be employed

17

there; a drunken man is unknown in the establishment,—a man who cannot trust himself hardly ventures to ask to be employed."

The above will shew clearly what a great amount of good can be secured by the intelligence and active benevolence of an individual. It is amongst one of the leading "signs of the times," and induces a hope that we are rapidly progressing towards a better feeling, and that common good will and understanding which should exist between the employer and the employed. It also clearly points out an effectual remedy for the vice and immorality which is now so loudly complained of.

Having thus far developed our general views on this subject, and without the most remote idea of assuming to dictate, we trust that the following suggestions will be received with that good feeling which we are so desirous of establishing.

In the first place we propose that proper steps should be taken in order to cause the removal of those who crowd the sleeping apartments, and whose occupations engender the noxious vapours complained of, to commodious and well ventilated shops. This would, in a great degree, tend to make the cottages of a great portion of the working classes of this town subservient to domestic purposes, and to a considerable extent remove the evils arising from the amalgamation of both sexes to which we have previously directed attention.

Secondly,—In order to effectually work out this praiseworthy object, we think it desirable to conciliate the good will and co-operation of the manufacturers, believing that even on pecuniary considerations they would find such an arrangement tend to their advantage, as well as confering a great public benefit in which themselves, as inhabitants of the town, would become participators.

Thirdly,—The propriety of applying to Parliament, or by a deputation, to the Government, requesting that any clause or clauses deemed necessary for carrying out the general question of sewerage, drainage, &c., should be introduced into the general act now contemplated by the Government, or to apply for a local act, if such should be considered necessary.

Finally,—That anything necessary to carry out the remedy which is contemplated, and which does not come within the immediate jurisdiction of Parliament, shall be provided for by the united efforts of the benevolent portion of the wealthier inhabitants by means of a general subscription for the purpose, and that the committee to carry out this important business should be partly composed of the wealthier classes.

We have great pleasure in announcing that the inhabitants of Leeds have cordially taken up this question, and that all classes and parties are united in working out this great blessing. A committee has been formed consisting of the Mayor, the Vicar, and other highly respectable gentlemen on the one hand, and by a number of intelligent working men on the other. This is a truly pleasing state of things; and we trust that this excellent example of Leeds, may be followed by the respectable portion of the inhabitants of Bradford. May this feeling go on and increase, and may the estrangement which has heretofore existed between the various classes of society, give place to nobler sentiments. We now leave the question to the discernment and humanity of the public; and feel convinced that all who read the facts set forth in this report, will conclude that the time has arrived when a great and comprehensive change shall take place in the condition of the working classes. And we sincerely hope that no interested or party feeling may enter into this question, in which the health and happiness of all are concerned.

On behalf of the Commmittee,

GEORGE WHITE, Secretary.

YORK WEST RIDING—TABLE OF MORTALITY.

Registration Districts.	Average age at Death of all who died.	Average age at Death of all who died above 20.	PROPORTION PER CENT. OF DEATHS, TO TOTAL DEATHS.													Proportion per cent. of Deaths to Births.	
			Under.				Between									Under.	
	yr. mth.	yr. mth.	1 year.	5 years.	15 years.	20 years.	20—30 years.	30—40 years.	40—50 years.	50—60 years.	60—70 years.	70—80 years.	80—90 years.	90 and upwards	1 year.	5 years.
Saddleworth, Ecclesfield, Wortley, & Ecclesall Bierlow.	26 3	52 10	23 8	43 2	52 0	55 6	8 0	6 0	5 5	7 0	7 6	6 6	3 5	0 3	14 0	25 4
Sheffield	22 6	51 6	25 4	49 7	56 7	59 9	6 6	6 1	6 7	6 0	6 1	6 3	2 1	0 1	16 7	32 7
Rotherham	28 5	54 6	23 9	33 5	45 8	53 1	8 4	5 6	4 4	7 5	8 4	7 4	4 7	0 4	13 5	18 3
Wakefield	30 5	53 11	21 1	35 2	42 6	46 9	9 1	6 8	8 1	5 7	9 3	9 3	4 2	0 6	12 7	20 4
Huddersfield	27 3	52 5	26 0	40 3	47 2	51 4	9 4	6 9	6 3	6 1	7 1	8 9	3 6	0 2	13 8	21 4
Dewsbury	23 6	52 0	28 2	46 2	53 6	59 0	7 7	6 6	5 6	4 9	6 4	5 7	4 0	0 3	14 1	23 2
Halifax	26 10	53 9	24 8	41 6	48 5	53 9	7 6	6 5	6 2	6 4	6 7	8 6	3 8	0 3	14 1	23 6
Bradford	20 3	50 7	29 5	50 8	58 9	64 6	7 7	5 2	4 5	5 3	5 1	5 2	2 3	0 2	17 0	29 6
Leeds	23 4	51 1	25 8	46 9	54 7	58 2	7 3	6 9	6 7	5 4	7 3	5 3	2 5	0 3	16 8	30 5
Otley and Keighley	28 5	54 11	25 8	40 1	46 9	51 7	8 7	7 1	5 0	5 3	7 1	7 6	6 5	0 9	14 9	23 2
Skipton, Sedburgh, and Settle	31 11	55 8	19 9	33 8	41 2	46 3	9 1	6 7	5 8	6 0	8 5	10 2	6 3	1 1	12 9	22 0
Pateley Bridge, Ripon, and Knaresboro	36 3	60 0	20 1	31 0	38 8	42 6	7 6	5 1	5 8	6 5	9 1	12 8	9 1	1 2	12 8	19 8
Selby Goole, and Pontefract	29 1	59 11	26 4	42 3	50 9	54 1	6 4	4 2	4 3	5 2	7 4	10 5	6 8	0 9	15 6	24 9
Thorne, and Doncaster.	32 5	58 2	20 0	34 5	44 1	47 6	6 8	6 5	5 7	5 4	8 6	11 6	6 6	1 2	13 4	23 2
Average	25 11	53 6	25 2	43 2	51 0	55 3	7 8	6 3	5 9	5 8	7 1	7 5	3 9	0 4	15 0	25 8
Total number of Deaths			6,161	10,580	12,495	13,554	1,903	1,527	1,440	1,425	1,738	1,831	967	107		

Extreme Districts.

	Pateley, &c.	Sheffield.
Total number of Adults prematurely dying......6295		
to every 10,000 of the population,......56	44	67
Number of all classes dying from Epidemic, Endemic, and contagious diseases......4343		
to every 10,000 population......39	23	51
Deaths of all classes from diseases of the respiratory organs......6227		
to every 10,000 of the population......55	34	74

EXCESS BEYOND THE LOSS OF LIFE EXPERIENCED PATELEY BRIDGE, RIPON, AND KNARESBOROUGH, PREVENTIBLE IN EACH DISTRICT.

Registration Districts.	Exces in number of			Year's loss of Life		Total loss of money value of productive labour, at 1s. per week, men, and 5s. per week, women, say 7s. per week to each adult individual	Total Loss on the Years' Deaths in				Approximate proportion of Life Lost by each Person.
	All Deaths	Dths. of Adults.	Births.	Every individual	Every Adult.		Sickness.	Funerals.	Labour.	Total.	
				yrs. mths.	yrs. mths.		£.	£.	£.		
Saddleworth, Ecclesfield, Wortley, & Ecclesall Bierley	331	113*	855	10 0	7 2	140	9,968	1,655	165,600	156,523	1-4th*
Sheffield	722	27	1,032	13 9	8 6	166	20,216	3,610	148,404	172,280	2-5ths
Rotherham	59	26*	188	7 10	5 6	107	1,652	295	28,569	30,516	1 5th*
Wakefield	150	50	406	5 8	7 1	138	4,480	800	71,070	76,350	1-6th
Huddersfield	219	63*	1,018	9 9	7 7	148	6,132	1,095	152,292	159,519	1-4th
Dewsbury	157	112*	775	12 0	8 0	156	4,396	785	79,092	84,273	1-3rd*
Halifax	266	96*	856	9 5	6 3	122	7,448	1,330	22,352	31,130	1-4th*
Bradford	696	271*	1,541	16 0	9 5	184	19,488	3,580	197,800	220,768	3-7ths*
Leeds	1169	104	2,014	12 11	8 11	164	32,732	5,845	317,028	355,605	1-3rd*
Otley and Keighley	73	658*	313	7 10	7 1	99	2,044	356	57,123	59,532	1-5th*
Shipton, Sedbergh, and Settle	107	25	138	4 4	4 4	64	2,996	535	32,704	36,235	1-8th
Selby, Goole, and Pontefract	181	44*	451	7 2	0 8	13	5,068	905	7,644	13,617	1-5th
Doncaster and Thorne,	105	59	279	3 10	1 10	36	5,432	970	19,620	26,022	1-10th
Total	4,334	528*	9,853				121,352	21,670	1,270,298	1,422,320	
Average				10 9	6 10	133					2-7ths*

* Diminution.

J. Ibbetson, Printer and Stationer, Bridge Street, Bradford.

Appendix

List of Woolcombers Submitted for Investigation by the Bradford Board of Guardians – 1854

Name	No. in family	Residence	Amount of income stated by Relief Committee	Amount of income stated by Board of Guardians
Manningham, Horton and Bowling Districts				
R. Edmondson	4	Broom St.	5/–	not known
P. Lawler	6	Broom St	8/–	12/6
M. Dunn	6	Broom St.	2/6	10/6
M. Dowley	7	Broom St.	7/–	8/10
J. Lynch	4	Broom St.	6/–	7/–
J. Connell	4	Broom St.	6/–	8/–
T. Gains	4	Broom St.	7/–	13/7
I. Gains	4	Broom St.	none	20/3
W. Johnson	9	Waddingtons Yd.	15/–	16/7
F. Magador	4	Broom St.	none	only 2 weeks unemployed
M. Lambert	7	Broom St.	8/–	30/3
D. Dickings	3	Bolling St.	4/6	10/8
T. Pickersgill	5	Bolling St.	none	12/2
R. Saunders		Waddingtons Yd.	will not be examined	
J. Conroy	3	Adelaide St.	none	3/3
H. Jackson	2	Adelaide St.	none	6/–
J. Fitzpatrick	4	Adelaide St.	4/6	13/–
P. Tool	4	Adelaide St.	none	11/2
R. Croft	5	Adelaide St.	7/6	12/–
J. Evens		Adelaide St.	none	found at work
J. Robinson	2	Adelaide St.	none	6/3
R. Hannah	3	Adelaide St.	2/–	3/–
W. Bryan		Adelaide St.	none	not known
M. Brewhatt		Adelaide St.	House locked up	
D. Casey	3	Peel St.	2/–	4/–
J. Casey	4	Peel St.	2/6	5/–
J. Kingdom	7	Peel St.	10/–	16/6
J. M'Cormack	7	Peel St.	8/–	10/–
B. Rourke	6	Peel St.	none	
D. John			not found	
J. Wilkinson	2	Harker St.	none	7/6
R. Broadbent	6	Manningham	6/–	12/–
M. Gatenby		Manningham	none	6/6
J. Brierley	2	Squire Lane	3/6	5/–
T. Ackroyd	11	Butterfield Houses	20/–	22/9
W. Hudson	5	Whitley St.	8/–	14/9

M. Stead	5	Burnley Fold	4/6	14/6
J. Long	4	Wilsons Row	none	8/6
M. Walsworth	2	Teetotal Row	4/7	
J. Nichol	4	Wood St.	2/6	5/–
J. Wood	4	Wood St.	6/–	18/–
T. Darsey	7	Wood St.	14/6	16/6
C. Sutton	3	Regent Sq.	none	11/–
G. Metcalfe	6	Regent St.	11/6	11/6
J. Farrar	3	Regent St.	none	2/–
J. Mackay	2	Regent St.	none	3/–
M. Ware	6	Regent St.	8/6	16/5
J. Copley	7	Regent St.	9/–	18/6
J. Murray	4	Regent St.	6/–	illegible
A. Pollard	4	Regent St.	sons working	
W. Ridge	2	Regent St.	in full work	

Bradford District

J. Dent	5	Thompson Alley	6/–	6/–
A. Milne	1	Thompson Alley	none	none
J. Denham	1	Thompson Alley	none	none
J. Carmody	1	Thompson Alley	none	found at work
C. Holt	8	Thompson Alley	11/–	12/6
J. Laycock	7	Thompson Alley	none	11/8
J. Sheridan	1	Prospect St.	none	1/6
T. Coulton	1	Victoria St.	none	working
M. Jordan	4	Victoria St.	none	none
P. Hartley	4	Victoria St.	4/–	7/–
J. Connor	5	Victoria St.	5/–	6/6
J. Quinn	7	Victoria St.	9/6	17/–
D. Whalen	4	Victoria St.	none	none
M. Carney	3	Victoria St.	1/6	1/6
R. Dunn	7	Victoria St.	8/–	
T. Mallon	1	Victoria St.	none	not found
P. Delaney	4	Victoria St.	6/–	removed
J. Delaney	4	Victoria St.	7/6	removed
J. Quinan	5	Thomas St.	none	1/6
P. Wallis	2	Victoria St.	3/–	3/–
J. Briggs	3	Chain St.	4/–	4/–
J. Wilson	1	Chain St.	none	none
J. Hirst	4	West End St.	2/–	8/–
J. Kelly	9	West End St.	17/–	17/–
H. Peacock	1	Longcroft Place	none	none
J. O'Donnell	1	Mill Bank	none	none
P. Ward	3	Mill Bank	none	none
T. Wright	1	Reform St.	none	back in work
W. Riley	5	Reform St.	8/–	8/–
L. Costegan	2	Reform St.	none	1/9
M. Dunn	6	Longcroft Place	9/–	15/6
M. Carberry	1	Longcroft Place	none	7/–

M. Carberry	1	Longcroft Place	none	none
G. Warriner	4	Longcroft Place	6/–	9/6
J. Keighley (Snr)	1	Black Abbey Fold	none	none
J. Keighley (Jnr)	5	Black Abbey Fold	7/–	7/–
J. Patterson	1	Black Abbey Fold	none	not in
P. Gilfoyle	2	Black Abbey Fold	none	7/–
T. Butler	7	Black Abbey Fold	12/–	13/6
P. Slavin	5	Black Abbey Fold	4/–	4/–
E. Kelly	4	Black Abbey Fold	none	not in
P. Cross	4	Boyes Court	7/–	8/–
H. Smollen	1	Boyes Court	2/–	2/6
J. Clear	1	Boyes Court	none	none
S. Donnolly	1	Boyes Court	none	3/6
T. Chester	1	Boyes Court	none	other family income
J. Thompson	4	Spink Place	5/–	7/–
T. Crabtree	1	Salt Pie St.	none	none
C. Keenan	1	Salt Pie St.	none	none
S. Davey	4	Salt Pie St.	9/–	6/–
P. Thornton	1	Salt Pie St.	working	
A. Barber	3	Salt Pie St.	4/6	6/–
S. Ball	4	Salt Pie St.	11/–	
H. Dobson	4	Salt Pie St.	6/–	3/–
W. Leighton	4	Salt Pie St	none	wife at mill
R. Appleyard	4	Low St.	4/–	7/6
G. Haworth	1	Low St.	1/6	4/–
J. Dearden	7	High St.		
T. Malone	1	Salt Pie St.	1/6	1/6 + loaf
J. Jackson	2	Hayworth St.	none	1/6
J. Cunliffe	6	Hayworth St.	10/6	10/6
J. Corkram	1	Providence St.	none	not in
F. Hunt	1	Providence St.	none	found at work
J. Bradley	1	Providence St.	none	found at work
M. Dunn	1	Providence St.	none	5/–
F. Parkinson	6	Providence St.	8/–	14/–
A. Adams	6	Providence St.	8/–	11/–
J. Shaw	9	Providence St.	10/3	21/6
J. Parker	2	Providence St.	7/–	8/–
J. Shackleton	5	Providence St.	8/6	8/6
W. Riley	7	Providence St.	10/–	11/8
B. Hartley	4	Grace Church St.	3/–	3/–
G. Shaw	8	Sedgewick St.	13/–	13/–
D. Cooper	6	King St.	2/9	not in
P. Lee	6	Thornton St.	3/–	3/–
T. Smith	7	Longlands St.	9/6	9/6
W. Pickles	4	Longlands St.	7/–	7/–
D. Connell	1	Longlands St.	none	found at work
J. Crowley	1	North Wing	4/–	4/–
S. Dunn	2	North Wing	2/–	5/–
T. O'Neill	5	North Wing	4/–	4/–
J. Whalen	2	North Wing	none	none

A. Harrison	1	North Wing	none	none
R. Halton	7	Philadelphia Ct.	7/–	38/–
J. Peel	6	Philadelphia Ct.	6/–	8/–
D. Lippey	5	Philadelphia St.	9/6	11/6
T. Ellis	3	Lilly Row	4/4	4/4
J. Burchett	1	Wapping Road	none	not in
J. Hunt	5	Ranter St.	none	not in
C. Dawson	3	Craven St.	none	8/–
W. Smith	5	Craven St.	7/–	8/6
J. Marshall	4	Ranter St.	6/9	9/5
S. Womersley	1	Wapping St.	none	1/3
T. Farrar	5	Wapping St.	3/6	5/5
R. Robinson	9	Wapping Road	14/–	19/–
J. Ellison	7	Wapping Road	7/–	12/4
J. Sutton	2	Wapping Road	none	not in
D. Arrall	3	Lilly Row	none	10/–
H. Pickles	7	North Wing	8/–	4/– + 8 loaves
J. Thornton	5	Paper Hall Ct.	7/–	3/6 + 7 loaves
J. Mann	5	King Charles Ct.	8/6	8/6
G. Cooney	1	Cavalier Ct.	none	1/6 + 2 loaves
E. Cooney	3	Cavalier Ct.	5/–	5/–
H. Binns	2	Park St.	none	not in
J. Palmer	1	Smithson Pl.	none	not in
W. Parker	2	Smithson Pl.	none	1/4
J. White	1	Smithson Pl.	none	removed
J. Sharp	3	Smithson Pl.	none	2/8
J. Wickwar	1	Wardle St.	none	none
B. Fieldhouse	9	Bolton St.	7/7	18/7
R. Carter	6	Garnett Sq.	8/6	8/6
J. Midgley	3	Barkerend	6/–	9/–
J. Brearley	4	Barkerend	6/–	7/–
T. Varley	3	Pit Lane	none	3/6
G. Edmondson	4	Pit Lane	6/–	not sure
M. Ownas	7	Pit Lane	5/–	5/–
A. Romaine	4	Pit Lane	none	1/3
J. Ryan	1	Pit lane	none	not in
E. Ryan	1	Pit Lane	none	not in
E. Seymour	5	Pit Lane	9/–	9/–
J. Leach	7	Pit Lane	4/5	10/11
J. Carr	4	Pit Lane	6/–	6/6
J. Farrar	8	Bradford Moor	14/–	13/6
J. Smith	2	School Sq.	none	not in
H. Wood	2	Daniel St.	2/6	2/6
J. Chesterton	3	Daniel St.	5/6	12/6
J. Gradwell	1	Daniel St.	none	none
P. Tweedale	6	Providence St.	10/–	10/6
E. Bergan	4	Providence St.	3/–	3/–
J. Bolt	5	Lees Yard	3/6	3/6
H. Rampling	5	Lees Row	9/–	9/–
J. Collison	9	Lees Row	13/4	16/6

J. Robinson	7	Back Hall St.	9/–	9/1
J. Carter	6	Hall St.	7/–	7/–
W. Smith	5	Hall St.	5/–	not in
A. Doyle	2	Mount St.	none	2/–
J. Cowell	4	Mount St.	5/–	8/–
R. Bland	3	Mount St.	3/–	3/–
W. Curtis	3	Lister St.	3/–	10/–
J. Naylor	7	Lister Row	12/–	20/6
T. Kitson	4	Cope St.	4/6	12/–
F. Payne	5	Cope St.	4/–	6/–
W. Gurney	6	Mount St.	4/6	6/3
M. Dunn	9	St Georges St.	6/–	10/–
J. Rice	1	Wellington St	none	removed
P. Dillon	2	Warwick St.	3/3	5/9
P. Carney	1	Warwick St.	none	not in
T. Darcy	4	Warwick St.	7/6	10/–
W. Savage	6	Warwick St.	10/3	
G. Payne	3	Warwick St.	8/6	got work
W. Stocks		Belgrave St.	4/–	not in
F. Hayes	6	Mount St.	7/6	removed
P. Dunn	4	Mount St.	6/–	
J. Hudson	1	Mount St	none	not in
F. Hudson	1	Mount St.	none	8/2
J. Oversby	6	Mount St.	8/–	10/–
W. Holgate	4	Mount St.	5/–	not in
W. Airey	5	Mount St.	8/–	14/6
W. Hudson	7	Mount St.	8/–	9/–
R. West	3	Mount St.	4/6	got work
J. Ingham	1	Mount St.	2/6	1/6 + 2 loaves
T. Kennedy	5	Barker Ct.	9/–	9/–
P. O'Brian	5	Bolton Rd.	8/7	11/6
J. Hall	6	Bolton Rd.	10/–	16/–
T. Haste	9	North Brook St.	12/9	15/6
J. Graham	9	Bolton Rd.	6/10	11/9
J. Bancroft	2	Bolton Rd.	2/–	
M. Hewitt	7	Bolton Rd.	4/–	12/–

Further Reading

Blythell, D., *The Handloom Weavers. A Study in the English Cotton Industry during the Industrial Revolution*, (CUP, London, 1969).

Briggs, A., *Victorian Cities*, (Odhams, London, 1963).

Burnley, J., *A History of Wool and Wool Combing*, (London, 1889).

Driver, C., *Tory Radical, The Life of Richard Oastler*, (Oxford University Press, Oxford, 1946).

Elliott, A., 'The Establishment of Municipal Government in Bradford 1837–57', *University of Bradford PhD Thesis*, 1976.

Engels, F., *The Condition of the Working Class in England*, (Granada, London, 1982).

Feather, G.A., *Oxenhope: A Pennine Worsted Community in the Mid-Nineteenth Century*, (Haworth Society, 1973).

Firth, G., *Bradford and the Industrial Revolution, An Economic History 1760–1840*, (Ryburn Publishing, Halifax, 1990).

Heaton, H., *The Yorkshire Woollen and Worsted Industry from the Earliest Times up to the Industrial Revolution*, (Oxford, 1920, 2nd ed. Oxford, 1965).

Hudson, P., 'Proto-Industrialisation: The Case of the West Riding Textile Industry in the 18th and early 19th Centuries', *History Workshop*, 12, 1981.

James, D., *Bradford*, (Ryburn Publishing, Halifax, 1990, Town and City Histories series).

James, J., *The History and Topography of Bradford*, (Longmans, London, 1841; centenary edition, Mountain Press, Queensbury, 1967).

James, J., *The History of Bradford and its Parish with Additions and Continuations to the Present Time*, (Longmans, London, 1866, reprinted by Mountain Press, Queensbury, 1967).

James, J,. *A History of the Worsted Manufacture in England*, (Longmans, London, 1857).

Jenkins, D.T. and Ponting, K.G., *The British Wool Textile Industry 1770–1914*, (Heinemann, London, 1982).

Lipson, E., *The History of the Woollen and Worsted Industry*, (London, 1921).

Mason, K.M., *Woolcombers, Worsteds and Watermills: Addingham's Industrial Revolution*, (Addingham Civic Society, 1989).

Peacock, A.J., 'Bradford Chartism 1838–40', Borthwick Institute of Historical Research, *Borthwick Papers*, no. 36, 1969.

Reach, A.B., in Aspin, C. (ed) *The Yorkshire Textile Districts in 1849*, (Blackburn Times Press, Blackburn, 1974).

Reynolds, J., *The Great Paternalist: Titus Salt and the Growth of Bradford*, (Maurice Temple Smith, London, 1983).

Richardson, C., *A Geography of Bradford*, (University of Bradford, Bradford, 1976).

Richardson, C., 'Irish Settlement in Mid-Nineteenth Century Bradford', *Yorkshire Bulletin of Economic and Social Research*, 20, 1968.

Roth, H., Hand Wool Combing, *Bankfield Museum Notes*, 6, 1909.

Scruton, W., *Pen and Pencil Pictures of Old Bradford*, (Thomas Brear, Bradford, 1889, reprinted by Mountain Press, Queensbury, 1968).

Scruton, W., *Bradford Fifty Years Ago*, (G.F. Sewell, Bradford, 1897).

Sigsworth, E.M., *Black Dyke Mills*, (University of Liverpool, Liverpool, 1958).

Smith, J., 'Report on the Condition of the Town of Bradford', *Health of Towns Commission*, Second Report, 1845.

Thornes, R.C.N., *West Yorkshire: A Noble Scene of Industry. The Development of the County 1500–1830*, (West Yorkshire Metropolitan County Council, Wakefield, 1981).

Ward, J.T., *The Factory Movement*, (MacMillan, London, 1962).

Wright, D.G., *The Chartist Risings in Bradford*, (Bradford Libraries and Information Service, Bradford, 1987).

Wright, D.G., 'Politics and Opinion in Nineteenth Century Bradford 1832–80', 2 vols, *University of Leeds PhD Thesis*, 1966.

Wright, D.G. and Jowitt, J.A., *Victorian Bradford*, (City of Bradford Metropolitan Council Libraries Division, Bradford, 1982).